AS ABOVE,

SO BELOW

Published by Jordan Stark

ISBN: 978-1-7375119-7-7 (paperback), 978-1-7375119-8-4 (hardback),
         978-1-7375119-0-8 (epub), 978-1-7375119-2-2 (audiobook)

186 pages, 15cm × 23cm (6in. × 9in.)

Keywords: Astrology, New Age, Spirituality, Health, Chakras, New Thought, Mysticism, Alternative Healing

Publishing and Design Services: Martin Publishing Services

AS ABOVE, SO BELOW

REDISCOVERING *the* SEVEN ANCIENT PLANETARY ARCHETYPES

☉ ☽ ♂ ☿ ♃ ♀ ♄

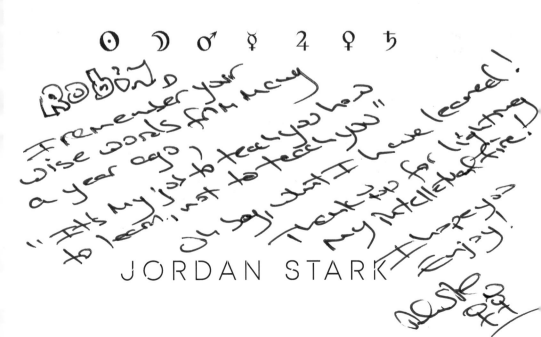

Robin,

I remember your wise words from many a year ago —

"It's my job to teach you how to learn, not to teach you."

Oh what I have learned!

Thank you for lighting my intellectual fire!

Always,

Enjoy!

JORDAN STARK

TO

my Mother

Mother Goose

and Mother Earth

"As above, so below,
as within, so without,
as the universe, so the soul…"

—HERMES TRISMEGISTUS

"When a child is born,
its heavens are born with it
and the seven organs which for themselves
have the power to be the seven planets
and thus everything that belongs to its heavens."

—PARACELSUS

"Your soul stands
under the influence of the planetary world:
Mercury, Jupiter and Venus,
Sun and Moon, Saturn and Mars.
Thus if psychology were to be studied,
the human being's vision was directed upward
to the secrets of the planetary world."

—RUDOLF STEINER

A very special thank you to
Dr. Robin Murphy, ND,
the "Bird Potato Man"

Thank you to
the KN Literary Team
for helping me put my dreams into reality

CONTENTS

PART I

PREVIEW TO THE ARCHETYPES

☉ ☽ ♂ ☿ ♃ ♀ ♄

INTRODUCTION

MONDAY'S CHILD

Monday's child is fair of face,
Tuesday's child is full of grace,
Wednesday's child is full of woe,
Thursday's child has far to go,
Friday's child is loving and giving,
Saturday's child works hard for a living,
But the child that's born on the Sabbath day,
Is bonny and blithe and good and gay.

—MOTHER GOOSE

AS ABOVE, SO BELOW: REDISCOVERING THE SEVEN ANCIENT PLANETARY ARCHETYPES will reveal the ancient lost secret of the seven days of the week, and the ways we have used them to interpret and understand human nature for millennia.

From the Mesopotamian cradle of life and the ancient Sumerian and Babylonian astrologers, to the early Jewish mystics and the Kabballah, to the times of the Egyptian pyramids and the lost Library of Alexandria, to the Persian, Greek and Roman Empires, to the Norse and Germanic cultures and languages and to China, Japan, India and the Incas, all of our great ancient civilizations named the seven days of the week after the same seven "naked eye" or visible planets, which they called their "Watchers," "Rulers," "Governors" or "Gods."

Why is this so? Why did every single civilization gravitate toward this same understanding? The answer is simple, as simple as the Mother Goose nursery rhyme that will send "mother goose bumps" down your spine when it is truly understood.

3

The answer lies in an ancient, lost system of astrology based on the seven days of the week, which align with the Seven Ancient Planetary Archetypes. These archetypes are eternal and personal, and they illuminate the way each of us enters the universe and journeys through it.

The very axis that our personalities, traits, and behaviors spin on, moves with the planet that rules us. If we are born on a Sunday, we are a "Sun" Planetary Archetype. Born on a Monday, a "Moon" Planetary Archetype; Tuesday, a "Mars" Planetary Archetype; Wednesday, a "Mercury" Planetary Archetype; Thursday, a "Jupiter" Planetary Archetype; Friday, a "Venus" Planetary Archetype; and Saturday, a "Saturn" Planetary Archetype.

Answers to the age-old question, "Who am I?" are as plain and straightforward as that—we are composed of the celestial bodies that guide us. But the depths of wisdom and life-changing consequences that can be gained from understanding these Seven Planetary Archetypes and their impact on our day-to-day choices, actions, and desires, are bottomless.

Reading through these pages, readers will come to realize how this ancient gnosis that has fueled my imagination for most of my life has been lost to time, but has been dwelling within us and acting upon our consciousness, regardless.

As Above, so below is set primarily in Maui, Hawaii, land of my childhood, setting of my soul, and place of deep mysticism and abundance. *Mahalo and Aloha.*

CHAPTER ONE

DISCONNECTION

TOO MANY SATELLITES AND STATIC

MAUI'S MONKEY POD TREES STAND ON THE PROPERTY I GREW UP ON with their branches outstretched, as if they are dancing and welcoming all mere Earthbound mortals to move closer, to let ourselves be embraced, and to climb. You can see the stuff of dreams from the heights of these trees, and I know this. If you climb high enough, you might end up in a rainbow. Whales breach and blow miles offshore in a show meant for your eyes only. Sparrows, mynas, waxwings, and doves swoop and dive for seeds you've scattered on your gentle journey away from terra firma.

As a kid, pulling all the scents of Hawaiian flora and fauna through my nostrils and deep into my lungs, I made it a regular mission to walk amongst and inside these trees. I spent time with them. I talked to them and befriended them. "I am you, and you are me," I would say.

"Whish, whish," they'd respond.

The adventures these trees promised and the truths that their stability offered, was irresistible to me. Shoeless, I placed one small dirty foot above the other and, stepping from one branch to another, I reached, literally, for the stars.

Even in the brightest sunlight, from my perch above the ground, I swore I could see the constellations, the planets, and the moons of moons. I couldn't, of course, but I did know where they were all located. In school, two of my favorite topics were outer space and Greek and Roman Gods and Goddesses. Living on Maui was paradise, and I always sensed powerful hidden spirits were near. In the dark night of my small town, far from light pollution, honking horns, and the swirl of humanity, I caught a thousand shooting stars, "who-whooed" back at owls, and had endlessly fascinating conversations with my family. Living on an island, I felt I possessed a unique

5

spatial awareness. A mix of stardust, Earth and ash, there I was, a kid in a tree on a mass of lush green-dipped black volcanic rock, some fourteen-hundred miles north of the Equator, spinning on a planet that was three hundred times smaller than the largest one—Jupiter.

I was lucky, and yet, I felt like a kid born way too late. Shy by nature, I still played all the games the other kids played. My sisters and I were like any other kids raised by parents who were in tune with Mother Earth; but still, even as a boy I sensed there was a time before time. I gobbled up my school lessons on Atlantis, the Olympians, the fossils of Colorado, the Great Pyramids and the Caduceus of Hermes.

Hermes, a God of many names, I learned, aided travelers. Did the tourists who flocked to the island I called home know to evoke him? When they stacked rocks on the beaches—making cairns of volcanic rock to mark their paths—did they know Hermes derived his name from the Greek word *herma*, meaning "heap of stones?" I would think about travelers and traveling often. In early adulthood, I would leave Maui, but I always returned home.

An old soul, maybe I have always been one.

The work of my soul has entailed, to some degree, sharing beauty, which in my mind, is born in an ancient and sacred place. I grew up on a steady diet of beach, sea, palm, gardenia, and the fruits and products my family grew and produced on our farm. My parents instilled in each of their children a fundamental appreciation for and knowledge of health and wellbeing. We knew the rough play of waves and the stillness of sunset. We attended a progressive small school and learned how to be civil and how to be ourselves there.

But so much of what I did have to teach myself—because the knowledge seemed hidden or forgotten, buried in some sinkhole on the road to Hana— seemed to be going in the opposite direction of society. That is, I watched Maui change over the decades, and saw it losing something. I saw too, that this change was happening all over the world—it was universal. Here we all were, these radical energetic clusters of everything that has existed since the dawn of time, and we had no clue how special and powerful we were.

We were lost.

Like the whale bombarded by too much military sea traffic noise.

We were hungry.

Like the feral cats of Kauai.

We were at risk of losing our home, Mother Earth, and our place on it.

Like the many native birds of Hawaii—the Kāma`o, the Kaua`I `ō`ō, and the Koa Finch—that have gone extinct thanks to rats, pigs, goats, invasive birds, and feral cats.

We didn't know who we were, and so our relationships with others and with the bigger picture—with time itself, time immemorial—were suffering.

We are suffering, to the point it feels we are de-evolving. All that has been done in the name of progress—on Maui and across the globe—has had consequences. So many of these consequences, we could not foresee—take plastic, for example. It changed how medicine, art, and science were done. But now we know we are not simply made of stardust, dirt, and ash. We are not made of sugar and spice and everything nice. We, like the whales, eat (and therefore are) plastic.

I am not one of those people who blames technology for the downward spiral of civilization, whether it came in the form of Tupperware in 1946 or the Internet in the 1980s. All mammoth, popular, or useful inventions, have their pros and cons. Nothing is black and white, ever. But the rate at which humanity has replaced valuable lessons from Pythagoras and Aristotle with vapid noise from televisions and reality TV stars, is startling. We have short memories, not because we are addicted to our cellphones, but because we live such a short spell on this planet, and it is easy—too easy—to forget what we are here for.

Defining who we are and what we are here for, for many, feels like a Herculean task. After working eight to ten hours a day, commuting one or two more, putting together a healthy and satisfying meal for dinner, and conversing thoughtfully with family or friends before bedtime, well . . . isn't that enough? No, it isn't.

Living solely in "it is what it is" mode is not enough. Research shows that people want, now more than ever, "something more," and that something more is not to be found online, in a thrift store, or in things.

The truth is, yes, *it IS what it is,* and that is all Zen and good and a mantra I actually believe in. But also, *it is what it always has been*—and this is the part I think we are missing out on. Not knowing our history and our deep history has consequences. Diabetes and heart diseases diagnoses are on the rise yearly. Anxiety disorders currently affect more than forty million people in the United States. A 2018 study conducted by Cigna used the UCLA Loneliness Scale and found that nearly half of people in the United States report "sometimes or always feeling alone." The $800 million self-help book publishing industry is growing at a rate of over 5% per year. People are clearly looking for solutions, answers, and light.

But there is hope. If we find our way back to the trees of our youth and to our respect for powers beyond and our own—if we scratch the surface that has been muddied by too much information and social media and distractions big and small—we can make ourselves whole again. We can ground ourselves by climbing a tree and looking out into space.

On Maui, I am constantly exposed to the power of the Mother Goddess. Lahaina, Maui, like many other locations on Earth, is a town under the influence of the Moon. This is a town that sleeps in the bosom of the Moon Goddess, drinking the intoxicating spirits of her silver milk. From scuba and snorkeling tours, to deep sea fishing excursions and submarine visits (or all things "sub/under") this town basks in a liquid lunar essence. A coastal town, tides ebb and flow here, and humans and animals must abide by this ancient and endless Moon-made rhythm. With its rich marine history, Lahaina has seen sailors from all lands come ashore only to lose their minds. People land in Lahaina, let the Moon take over, and become lunatics!

Or, like me, they sit under the Great Banyan Tree and breathe.

The Great Banyan Tree—the oldest *paniana* tree in Hawaii and the largest in the United States—lives in Lahaina, on the western, or dark side, of Maui. Beneath its seventeen trunks, I sit and prepare to meditate. I sit, as I like to call it, in "three-legged praying mantis" position (a praying mantis with three of its four bottom legs), or all "kapakahi," lopsided and out of balance, like an imperfect human being, because just like all other human beings, I too, am a work in progress. I am learning, growing, and evolving and it is okay to be a three-legged praying mantis, as long as we are trying— trying to meditate or trying to reach beyond the world we walk through sometimes too carelessly, toward greater self-realization.

Under this great tree, I let my thoughts and emotions move in and out—like the tides—and I practice the lost art of meditating on the Sound.

The Sound has been known by many names, first and originally, the Ancients called it the "Sound Current," the "Audible Life Stream," or the "Thought." In various religious circles, the Sound was known as the "Word," and then for some, "the word made flesh." In science, it is called the "Big Bang." It is also known as Mana, Chi, Tao, and so on. A Zen proverb says, we can "knock on the sky and listen to the Sound."

Whatever we choose to call it, the Sound emanates from a place of zero negativity, and therefore brings calm and peace. I like to call what I'm sitting under the Great Banyan tree communing with, "the Verse," the verse of the Universe.

If we want to begin to remedy our disconnection to ourselves, to one another, and to Mother Earth, we must all sit with patience. By a tree, a river, the ocean, or simply in a small corner of our home we have carved out for ourselves, we can shut out the static of our daily lives—the literal static that buzzes from all of our appliances and the figurative static that consists of all the things we convince ourselves we should be doing instead of sitting in stillness.

Seated, we can practice humility in meditation, dissolving our thoughts, words, and actions into no thoughts, no words, and no actions. There is only the Sound, the Thought, the Word of God, the Verse. And there, or here, for me, for you, for your neighbor or the stranger across the planet, by clearing out our human soul space, we realize the Macrocosm, the Heavens, or the As Above and all the Planetary Gods and Goddesses watching over us. They are fueling and feeling us; moving and settling us; they are us! Scientists tell us that we are made of the same cells, elements, molecules, atoms, and metals of the universe and the seven planets. We are!

But even long before we had the technology to hook up to the human body and brain and study its mysteries and transmissions, we knew about mysteries. We were in many ways, closer to what our eyes (still) cannot see. The Ancients believed in the Seven Planetary Gods as "Watchers," "Rulers" or "Governors" who ruled human Destiny and Fate. This wisdom was carried forward for a spell, and then lost. Now that we have found it again, we can call on the Seven Ancient Planetary Archetypes to help us diagnose how we are created in the image of our Creator, and more importantly who and why we are. By "meditating with planets," the original satellites, and getting to know their Soul, their Essence, their Tinge, their Intelligence, and their Symbol, we can better know ourselves and others.

There may be hundreds of human built satellites crossing the skies above my head in Maui in any given hour. These instruments roam the universe in search of other life; they allow us to use our GPS systems, radios, and cellphones; they allow us to tune in, live stream, and binge watch whatever we want, whenever we want to. Relying on GPS, on Google, on the Internet, I am not judging, but we can reduce our reliance on this type of relationship so that we can come back to the relationships that matter most, that matter more.

As Above, so below, as in Heaven, so on earth. Macrocosm and microcosm!

The trees of my youth and the Great Banyan tree in Lahaina have, like Shel Silverstein's *The Giving Tree*, offered me their fruit, their wisdom, and so much more. These trees are still alive and healthy, but so many aren't. Too many trees have given too much of themselves. (So much for technology helping us cut back on our use of paper, right?)

The branches of the banyan reach out horizontally in a way that boggles the mind—what about gravity? The banyan's branches are almost a mirror image of its roots. They are long and extensive; they are life receiving and life giving. All trees, regardless of shape or stature, represent our ancestry, our roots, our beginning and our first and original knowledge.

When I am with trees, it is clear to me that they have seen the human race come and go. Sitting in Lahaina, watching tourists come and go; I look up at the Moon. It is empty of people, and one week after being as full and as bright as an aluminum mixing bowl in a baker's kitchen, it is rising over the ocean to bathe thousands of couples who have traveled from afar for romance. As the Moon continues its cyclic journey to becoming a new Moon, I contemplate the relationship between dark and light and being asleep versus being awake.

Our ancient knowledge—from alchemy, astrology, philosophy, mathematics, religion, language, and science—has been veiled in darkness, but it is returning. We know that the Sun and Moon affect us, but so do Mercury, Venus, Mars, Jupiter and Saturn. Let's turn toward knowing where we stand—or where we sit and listen and breathe—in relation to these spinning bodies. Let's remember all myth comes from a seed of truth—there are Gods and Goddesses everywhere.

As a boy at the Haleakala Waldorf School, our main morning lessons revolved around Greek, Roman and Norse myths. I drew many sketches and wrote stories of Apollo, Artemis, Ares, Hermes, Zeus, Aphrodite, and Chronos. I also spent time devouring images and tales of other ancient Gods and Goddesses from other cultures around the world. What they did above—I either witnessed or performed on my own stage of life, below. As I journeyed into adulthood, I knew how easy it would be to get caught up in the rigamarole. What many of us are expected to do, even if we have been raised in a remote place by "alternative-thinking" parents and Waldorf teachers, is: Go to college, get a job, find a partner, and have children. Work hard. Retire. And die.

There is nothing wrong with realizing and basking in joy at each and any of those waypoints, but on this voyage we must not lose sight of the planets that guide us, that offer us a map for living in a way that aligns fully with our own unique and powerful purpose.

Who am I and why am I here?

You cannot Google the answers to such questions.

CHAPTER TWO

RECONNECTION

WITHIN AND TO ONE ANOTHER

I F HERMES WERE ALIVE TODAY, I BELIEVE HE WOULD CHOOSE TO LIVE— as my mother did after watching Jimi Hendrix's *Rainbow Bridge* filmed on Maui—in Hawaii. The word "Hawaii" is derived from *Ha,* meaning breath of life, *wai,* meaning fresh water or water of life, and *I,* or God and Consciousness. Hermes would live here, on the top of the world, next to volcanoes and fire, inside stories-high waves and lyrical winds, and amongst flowers of the brightest hues and fragrances, because here, one can more easily diagnose the Word, the Sound, the essence of the universe and one's place in it. Here, one can sit, breathe, and reach out, as the branches and roots of the great banyans do, to another who is equally interested in listening for and discovering what has been lost in the insane rush of busyness. Hermes was the original grounder, connector, networker, and fortunately, his energy is ever-present, everlasting.

In this fertile, secret-holding and secret-sharing land, waters run deep with ancient knowledge and wisdom. They run to us, over us, and past us from a time before time. Whether you have stepped foot on one of the Hawaiian Islands or not, you have no doubt heard of its myths and wonders. Many of us who grew up on the islands, whether Kanaka Maoli, Native Hawaiian, or not, understand there are spaces and places where ancient knowledge and wisdom is stored and where it slips through the cracks, literally, between rocks, tree roots, and blades of grass. It spills out of rainbows. It gushes over steep cliffs in the form of waterfalls.

Walking now through my childhood haunts in Maui, or in similarly spiritual places such as Sedona, Arizona, I continually ask myself why, in the modern world, we are not paying enough attention to how our earliest ancestors lived. In school, we studied what they believed in, and yet, how quickly we forget or dismiss their minds and spirits. How quick we are to draw a line of accepted history at one particular place in the sand. But for me, there is value in looking backwards, above, beyond, beneath, ahead, and here, now. I understand time as a container for all of time, and as a container for the fact—the scientific and mystical fact—that we are stardust.

I was raised by a woman who was ahead of her time. My mother studied homeopathy and naturopathy starting in the '70s. She knew how to use herbs and remedies. She was well learned in diet and nutrition, vitamins, and minerals. She practiced acupuncture. When I had a cold, she placed two small needles in my earlobes or on either side of the bridge of my nose. She brewed lemongrass tea we grew in our garden, and the scent of it permeated our pores. Her balms and psalms healed us.

My mother instilled in me an understanding of what I would eventually call the "Five Elements of Health," or the five things that we can live the least amount of time without: Air/Breath, Water/Fluids, Earth/Diet, Fire/Movement, and Space/Thought.

My mother influenced my attitude and my siblings toward cultivating the land and living off it. We learned at a visceral fingers-in-the-dirt level how to take and how to give back. My chores were tending our garden, composting, and cutting our three-plus acres of kukui nut grass. On our citrus farm, we grew lemons, cherries, oranges, bananas and various other fruits. We plucked and ingested fruit almost daily from our very own Garden of Eden.

As a white child, a haole, on Maui, I was considered a little bit "out there," even in the '70s and '80s. This was a classification that was sometimes hard to accept, but usually impossible to deny. We were a mostly vegetarian family, and in elementary school, I was always trying to swap my cream cheese and alfalfa spout sandwich for a ham or Spam sandwich. I was never successful. When we had friends over, my sisters and I tried to hide our "weird" organic foods and sodas from them, not because we were stingy with food, but because we knew their parents bought them regular junk food and sodas, and we didn't want the secret to get out—we were really *really* different.

Of course, we did many of the usual natural and wild things kids do. We explored caves, swam for hours in the sea, and built forts. We wove headpieces and baskets out of palm fronds. We played pirates and deserted islanders. We surfed and bodysurfed. But we also attended Sufi camp with my mother. Wavy Gravy, peace activist and official clown of the Grateful Dead, taught me how to juggle at one of these camps. Growing up, my fingers may have been in the dirt of Maui, but my head was definitely in the clouds. And clouds above islands, as you know, move rapidly and shapeshift often.

My childhood was unique, but balanced. My imagination was rich and limitless. My teachers drew me into the world of art, science, and mythology without a fight. Even in high school, when I turned into somewhat of a rulebreaker, I loved to study. Between some of my more alternative explorations of the mind, I read voraciously about ancient Gods and Goddesses, and about the journeys they took and guided others on. I traveled often via the Word, and Hermes was a copilot whose story I returned to again and again. With each visit, he grew in my esteem, and my understanding of the construction of a universe based on As Above, so below developed.

As an adult, I would learn about another Hermes, Hermes Trismegistus of Egypt, who was the original "Scribe from Heaven," and who would become one of my favorite and most influential muses in my museum of muses. The Staff of Hermes, or the Caduceus, symbolizes in the modern world: health, medicine and physicians. My mother passed away in this modern world, in a hospital bed that was surrounded by modern machines and technology, but she was a woman who had long studied human health. She lived, breathed, and promoted us knowing ourselves deeply, so that we could do what we were put on this earth to do. She lived well and she died well. She was instinctively and inherently connected to Hermes and to the Caduceus.

We have forgotten what the symbol of the Caduceus means, how, at its most fundamental level, it represents the teachings of Hermes Trismegistus, the ancient principle of As Above, so below and the ancient knowledge, wisdom and science that must be relearned and remembered if we are going to evolve and continue with our place here on earth. If we look to this symbol, to the snakes curving around the staff and meeting at seven distinct points, we can see how it might direct us in our efforts to renew our connections—to relearn and relove what is contained within us, our DNA. We can sit beneath a tree, close our eyes, meditate and listen for the Word, or the Sound. We can simply be. And then we can open our eyes, rise to our feet, and carry our peace and energy out into the world, for others to bask and grow in.

The very DNA of energy, health, and unity is represented in Hermes' staff. Hermes believed and taught that within the universe, there lies a hidden or "sidereal" force that shines and flows from the stars and celestial bodies to form the spiritual Man, our Astral Spirit, our Soul—or the primordial essence of who we are. This soul is in direct relationship with the stars, or planets, from which it was born. This soul is in harmony, vibration, and resonance with this great big round body, spinning and revolving, sometimes many light years away—but eternally there, and always communicating.

We rely on satellites, email, GPS, SMS, you name it now to relay our urgent and our inane messages. We are caught in this World Wide Web, these social networks, but beneath, above, beyond, and over it all, as Hermes knew, there is the Word Wide Web. The Word is constantly bounding toward us, making an effort, looking to enlighten and connect us to what really matters.

So, what really matters?

Who are you? Who am I? Who are we together and what and why are we here? How did this one planet become our home?

Hawaii is often in the news, not only for its world-renowned surf contests and active lava flows, but for stories of protection of its flora and fauna and its native sacred sites and peoples.

For decades, tourists have traveled the beaten path, beating it further to its current state, where much of it is endangered, or in danger. Whale migration paths have been permanently disturbed by military missions and by a general increase in sea traffic. Hundreds of invasive plant and animal species have taken control of some valleys, completely changing the landscape and the balance and health of it. Hikers go missing and when they are found alive, there is of course, celebration; but, for native Hawaiians whose sacred lands have been sometimes been denigrated by those who are lost, there is mourning. As the popular saying goes, it's complicated.

It seems increasingly complicated, everywhere we go, to stay calm and to stay the course. It feels challenging to take the time to take care of ourselves, let alone others and our Mother, Earth. But we must make the time and the effort to open ourselves back up so that the very air we breathe can flow through us, energize us, and connect us. We live in shocking times, but instead of cracking us open toward more understanding and unity, some of us are shutting down. Isolating. Forgetting even further where we came from and how powerful we can be.

When I was a seven-year-old boy living in Hana, I cracked my head open. It was an accident, of course—I'd been hanging on to the back of our Jeep, playing "Rat Patrol", a TV show I enjoyed as a child, and when we pulled into our garage to park, I fell. My head hit the garage post first, and then the rough cement. My family thought I was dead, and I have a distinct memory—as cliché as it sounds—of floating above my body and seeing myself splayed out there. I can't explain where I might have gone to this day, but I do know that family friends who owned a funeral home ended up driving me along the Hana "highway" to the hospital, in their hearse.

Did the head injury I sustained and healed from color the way I moved forward in the world? In those few seconds of hovering above my own little limp and unconscious body, did I enter the realm of the Gods—the realm I'd enjoyed studying so early on in school? I hope so. I believe so.

I also believe that, fortunately, we do not have to sustain a head injury or other trauma to access the Gods and the Goddesses that guide us. We can begin to harmonize and align with the As Above, so below principle in order to improve our own health and wellbeing, by studying (again, and in an ancient but new way) the universe.

Hermes believed that the human race was created in the image of the Creator, and therefore, we must also be creators. We create in infinite ways, but in the same way as our Creator, via "thoughts" and with our "words." As we think, or as we use words to convey meaning and to mirror and build what we perceive of as reality, we are actually creating an illusion. We can't help sometimes getting too caught up in this cycle though (for we are "only human"), and that is why meditation, walking or sitting in nature, and taking time out to listen and focus on our breath is necessary.

In a meditative state, or in prayer, as our thoughts flow to us and through us—like lava—our mind clears and the veil recedes. We slip back into the ancient, original, and eternal stream of consciousness, and we reconnect with our Creator. We become whole, One, and All. In this state, we have no limitations. Our beloved has no limitations; our neighbor has no limitations. Anything is possible, and it anything has always been possible since the dawn of time, since the Big Bang created the universe and the Gods and Goddesses planted the Garden of Eden. Any way you look at it and whatever you believe, we come from the same source. Any confusion or troubles we are sensing, we are experiencing because we have diverged and forgotten. We have traveled far, but we are never as far from what we need or know as we've been tricked into thinking we are. Hope is never lost, even if we are. Find your own banyan tree, sit with it, and listen.

The fall I took off my family's Jeep as a boy was not the last time I would injure my head and travel to the invisible astral world. I found over and over again, via boyhood mishaps and manhood explorations, the mysterious, hidden spark, the ether and the 5th element. I have consciously set out to break through the static and my own routines and habits to observe, search, and pay attention.

After my potentially fatal fall on our Hana property, my family became spooked. We connected the mishap to the two large tiki statues we had recently purchased. We also learned that the house was built on a heiau, a Hawaiian sacred temple site where ancient Hawaiians worshipped and made sacrifices to their Gods and Goddesses. Unsettled, we moved to another house in Hana. It too felt somewhat inhabited by something otherworldly, not of an earthbound plane.

In the second Hana house was a staircase that made a left turn to the second level. In the dark, the angle the stairs took made them appear to lead directly into the wall, and I always felt that beyond that wall, dwelled something unknown and mysterious. Every time I went upstairs, I shivered a bit, feeling like I did whenever I stared into the full moon, wondering if I could jump through the silvery white hole in the sky to see what was on the other side.

I was convinced the house was haunted, but rather than fear the Night Marchers or the White Lady, I chose to focus on the atrium at the top of the house, where birds circled constantly. I chose to focus on the positive forces—what was in flight, what was taking to the sky, what was capable of respecting and erasing the boundaries of As Above, so below. After a couple of years in Hana, we flew the coop and moved to the small north shore town of Haiku, the place of the monkey pod trees and the place I will always call my home.

21st Century space scientists take us to the planets via satellites and rovers, and via close-up photographs we never could have imagined anyone taking and processing just decades ago, when Neil Armstrong took one small step onto the Moon. Our quest to know our universe more intimately continues to evolve, and what we are learning now of lost seas, hidden valleys, and life-sustaining gases illuminates, in my mind, the ancient terrain we carry within.

The seven planets have "thoughts," or energy, and in stillness or moments of calm and clarity, I can feel their cosmic butterfly effect. I was born on a Friday, and Venus is my ruling planet, her thoughts breathe life into me, mentally, emotionally and physically. Knowing the day of the week we were born on and the ties we have to the planet ruling that day, in my mind, enlarges our capacity as human beings. Knowing ourselves from within, so that we can fulfill our unique destiny without, during our brief time on this planet is a duty—to ourselves, to our friends and loved ones, and to our Creator.

CHAPTER THREE

CONNECTION

TO OUR CREATION STORIES,
TO MOTHER EARTH, AND TO THE UNIVERSE

MANA, ALSO KNOWN AS SPIRITUAL ENERGY OR LIFEFORCE, EXISTS IN every rock, flower, waterfall, and animal—human beings, included—on the Hawaiian Islands. I encounter mana in my current home state of Arizona. I find it in Colorado and every state that I have lived in or been to. Mana is everywhere; it is Mother Earth herself.

Through prayer, meditation, and the setting of our intentions, we call upon mana. We can touch mana and benefit from all the Goddess-Godly powers it possesses by consciously choosing to escape the every-day static of our busy lives and the constant push to "achieve," be movers and shakers, and multitask. Wherever we are, we can take a moment to close our eyes, focus on our breath, and cross the invisible membrane that too many people assume "separates" us in our day-to-day mundane perceptions and the otherworldly realm. We are one with this realm. There is no division other than the one in our minds. Each of us is part human/animal, part obsidian/gardenia, part prism/dew drop, and part salt fleck and song. We are mantra, ocean wave, and planet. Our DNA, in all its infinitude, carries the Gods, Goddesses, and demigods we originally sprouted from.

Maui, son of the God, ʻAkalana, and the Goddess, Hina of Hilo, was a Polynesian demigod. We are all part Maui.

Born prematurely, Maui was not an easy infant to handle, and his mother—guardian of the path to the invisible world—cast him into the Pacific Ocean. Beneath the sea, he was befriended and cared for by jellyfish, whales, and sea Gods. In boyhood, while legend varies as to which Polynesian island became his first earthly home, he ventured onto land and began to merrily and mischievously entertain himself with the sun, the birds, and the wind. Maui was small, and after playing pranks that often benefitted humankind—for example, he stole fire from a flock of wise birds and gave it to us—he would shapeshift, turn himself invisible, disappear. Maui's mercurial nature, his keen powers of observation, and his ability to take on any form, allowed him to wander the sea, the earth, the sky, and the underworld, seamlessly.

The long light-filled days in Hawaii are brought to us by Maui, who, in his eternal fascination with fire, not only toyed with the sun, but harnessed it atop Haleakala, the House of the Sun, to slow it down.

With the very same sacred bone fishhook he used to capture and control the sun, one day, it is said, he set out to prove himself to his brothers and ended up creating the Hawaiian Islands (or more of them, there are over one hundred total in the archipelago). All skilled fishermen who mocked Maui for his stature and lack of fishing prowess, the brothers finally relented to his nagging and allowed him onto their canoe. They did not know he had baited his powerful hook with a type of bird that was magical to their mother, an Alae. Hina did not know this either, but when she found out, she rushed to her sons' boat.

By the time Hina arrived, it was too late. Maui had dropped his enchanted line to the bottom of the sea two days prior, and the boys had been struggling day and night to keep the line taut. The boys were committed to their prey and would not follow their mother's order to let go. They wanted to capture a load of fish bigger (and heavier) than they had never caught before!

Two versions of what happened next exist: One, either Maui warned his brothers not to look behind them at their catch, much like Hades and Persephone warned Orpheus not to turn back toward Eurydice. But one brother, in his anticipation to see the silver, red, and black fish he believed were on the line, did look, and this caused the thousands of fish in tow to turn into islands; or, in version two, when Hina found her sons, she reached into the sea to grab for her bird, and caught only a portion of its wing. This tore the feathered beast apart, so instead of it resurfacing as one intact land mass, it broke into pieces—it became islands.

Maui stole from birds, he turned one of his mother's birds into the world's most isolated island chain, and he also transformed birds from invisible to visible. We see the Nene, the I'iwi, and the Akiapolaau now, while before Maui used his powers, ancients only felt them rustling and fluttering by, or heard them singing. This swift demigod, who is sometimes called the Mercury or the Hercules of Hawaii, truly gave wing to winged things.

Did my mother choose Maui for us, or did Maui choose us? As a boy, I was also mercurial and lightning fast, athletic, mischievous, and a quick study. My mind still races, and I sometimes wish I could carve and consecrate a bone or shell hook like Maui's, to harness my thoughts. I would like to make what we cannot see, visible. Maui lifted the skies from the Earth so that mere mortals would have more room to flourish and grow. When I climbed those trees as a kid and when I sit beneath them now and feel their roots and branches mirrored in my lungs and the air I inhale and exhale, I am aware of how Hina's prized Alae transformed itself and each plant and tree has space to fill.

When I watch windsurfers at Ho'okipa, I remember that Maui was the first weatherman, of sorts, and his inventiveness and curiosity in the wind led to helping us organize and plan. He built a kite of *kapa* cloth, which his mother was a master of making, and ancient people learned that when the kite flew steadily, the weather would remain agreeable. They would then plan outdoor work schedules and activities.

But of course, we can all harness Maui, or Mercury, or Hercules, if we want to. Each of us can realize what we are made of, we can reach for the stars and ingest their light, and we can make choices that are based in ancient wisdom and ritual to help assure the eternal recycling and evolution of our souls.

We have been living with what Malcolm Gladwell termed the "the tipping point," or the era of critical mass, for decades now. Raised as I was by my mother, I presaged some of what Gladwell preaches. I paid attention to my surroundings and to all sentient beings, including the planetary bodies continually circling overhead. I was taught at a very early age to watch what I put into my body in terms of food, and what I put into my mind in terms of thoughts. And there too, I recognized a connection—we are what we eat, and vegetables are food for thought. I saw firsthand what it meant to slaughter, consume, and waste animals. To feed animals that would feed us was "double-feeding," and that system was never going to be sustainable.

In thinking short term and forgetting how our ancestors and our great-great ancestors lived and worshipped according to the movement of the planets, the sun, and the moon, we are destroying our planet. When we separate ourselves—consciously or unconsciously from the bodies that rule us—we destroy our bodies, as well as our souls, our spirits, and the entire universe. We are stardust and the marvelous energy of all our planets, but now we are also hormones, pesticides, plastics, and a general trickling down of the sum of our lifestyle choices and practices.

But what if we could begin to know ourselves and heal ourselves and our planet by following our own version of Hina, the mother with the gift of navigating As Above, so below?

My mother had a teacher I also learned from, directly and indirectly, I call him the Bird Potato Man. Mom studied homeopathy with him, so did I, and he became one of the most important male influences in my life. He held the sky up for me, breathed more space into my world, and encouraged me to delve deeper into the mysteries of the planets. In my later years, I studied all of his healing and homeopathy courses. And I never forgot what he once said to me: "It is my job to teach you how to learn, not to teach you."

The Bird Potato Man, like Maui, lit a fire.

When I collected seashells or sliced open a deep purple beet from our garden, I noted a spiral. A small crab carried the universe, its home, on its back—and the spiral that housed it permitted it to grow without changing shape. The beets that nourished us with nitrates and traces of soil, strengthened our brains and bones and helped circulate more oxygen through our bodies. We dined on the atmosphere, and it fueled us. Even when the atmosphere was agitated, hurricane satellite imagery showed a perfect storm building, in the shape of a Fibonacci Spiral. Our Milky Way Galaxy, with its stars as old as the universe, was another wild spiral of my night dreams. Each birdsong or rock love ballad was composed of a blend of keys on a scale, to create a harmony. Everything I touched, saw, heard, tasted, smelled, or puzzled over, was part of a large orbiting phenomenon and I wanted to tap into and connect all the dots.

Mom's friend and guide did teach me to ask questions and approach all that I learned from fresh alternative angles. I put myself in other people's shoes, but I also made an effort to approach the unknown, or a challenge, via multiple points of view. I could see myself as one small dot, a mere speck, on Maui, in the middle of the Pacific Ocean, on Earth, in the solar system as we knew it then and know it now. I was tiny and powerful, important and insignificant, wise and naïve. Always, I was being moved and guided by mana, Gods, Goddesses, demigods, and the ruling planets, or my Watchers. There was never a day I was not involved in some sort of dance, slow and barely perceptible, or raging and wild, with the universe.

As a Planetary Being, a man on and of Earth, the full moon and the high tide fill me. When the moon wanes and the tide recedes, activity stills. I kick my feet up and read a book. The hermit crab retreats into its homes and burrows below the surface, As Above, so below, in an act that amounts to layering darkness upon darkness upon darkness, in yet another spiral upon spiral. During a total solar eclipse, the sun and the moon, for several sacred seconds, appear to be the same size, a celestial and harmonious dance for our eyes only. The temperature drops, tiny crescent-shaped light patterns jitterbug on sidewalks, and birds stop singing.

And then there is Venus, my planet, the only one named after a female, a Goddess. She is the brightest body above us after the sun and moon, and she rotates opposite most other planets. She's my Watcher, and though she is covered in clouds, hidden and secretive, I find comfort in always being able to find her. Venus is the Earth's watcher too, absorbing heat from the sun like no other planet does. What we do learn of her, we need to learn quickly, because with her hot surface and temperament, even our best scientific equipment melts. If I could tolerate 800+ degree temperatures and stand on one of her mountain ranges, I would witness the sun rising in the west and setting in the east. In my meditations, I do this. Hot storms of dense gases swirl around me, and all I can feel is love and beauty.

We continue to look to the sky, and though the science of the universe has certainly evolved and our equipment is engineered to fly further, orbit longer, land on and sample from more extreme and hostile environments, the mystery and magic of what's out there is what inspires me most. I want to know, I don't want to know, and somehow, I just know, because everywhere I look, I find things to be As Above, so below. There is other life out there, it knows we are here, and though its air and its water, its tiniest microbes and its widest valleys differ from ours, this life is connected to our life. The planets that rule us, rule it. We may feel particularly vulnerable now, alone on our planet and making a mess out of it, but if we can each find a tree, plant a tree, connect our souls to the ancient messages, we can turn our world around.

Understanding more about the web we are part of will motivate us to heal it. Understanding more about ourselves—who is your Watcher, which planet should you turn toward and bask in—fuels us to do more of what we were born into this universe to do.

CHAPTER FOUR

THE ANCIENT AGE
AND THE POWER OF SEVEN

D OZENS OF "SEVEN WONDERS" LISTS EXIST, BUT THE ORIGINAL AND MOST well-known list is the "Seven Wonders of the Ancient World," which is comprised of the Great Pyramid of Giza, the Hanging Gardens of Babylon, the Temple of Artemis at Ephesus, the Statue of Zeus at Olympia, the Mausoleum at Halicarnassus, the Colossus of Rhodes, and the Lighthouse of Alexandria.

Acts of God, such as floods, earthquakes, and fires—or conquering societies simply demolishing works they found irrelevant and recycling valuable materials—have laid flat each of these classical wonders, save the Great Pyramid. But living on into perpetuity is the notion that the number seven represents a state of perfection, efficiency, or luck. Seven is something to pay attention to, to understand and have knowledge of!

Before we die, we are encouraged to fulfill our bucket lists. Depending on our passions, we could visit what the American Society of Civil Engineers have decided are the Seven Wonders of the Modern World. We could visit the Seven Wonders of the Middle Ages, the New Seven Wonders, or the Seven Natural Wonders of the World. As someone who travels frequently, I am a fan of any list that promotes exploration, awe, and honor. I am also someone who sees beauty, magic, and the number seven everywhere I look.

Seven of Hawaii's eight main islands are permanently inhabited. There are Seven days of Creation and seven days in the week. There are seven classical planets and their seven associated metals. There are seven continents and seas. There are seven virtues and sins. There are seven colors—ROYGBIV— in a rainbow. There are seven notes—ABCDEFG—in a musical scale. In Las Vegas, a city that prides itself on following no laws of nature other than the seediest and most sinful, spinning three sevens brings the "sound of rain"—meaning a player has hit the jackpot and coins are flowing their way.

Seven holds potential, power, purpose, and prayer. One ancient scroll, *The Book of the Hidden Chamber*, documents lessons on how to carry on bravely above ground, and how transcend our inevitable entry into and passage through the underworld. It is a document I would place near my As Above so below bookshelf. Sketched some two thousand years ago on a papyrus belonging to Nesmin, a priest who wore amulets of Thoth on each wrist and served Min, the God who created all Gods and humans in this text, we see the sun God, Ra, moving through the twelve hours between sunset and sunrise. In the seventh hour, as he begins to turn from the deepest darkness to regenerate, he meets Apophis, a huge and terrifying serpent. In this hour, even this great and powerful God must conquer his fears and call for assistance.

Ra gets help, obviously, which is why night still turns into day. But the lesson is this: In our seventh hour, when order and chaos, potential and resistance collide, if we want to survive, transform, and usher forth light again, we must rally our allies and not back down. Ra's seventh hour showdown story might be harsher than what I normally enjoy, celebrate, or share, but there is no denying we should be alert to what is to come after one, two, three, four, five, and six!

Sunday, Monday, Tuesday, Wednesday, Thursday, Friday, and Saturday: The seven days of the week have been used to guide, interpret, organize, classify, and understand human nature for millennia. Why is this so? Why did every single civilization gravitate toward this same understanding? The answer might be as simple as the "Monday's Child" nursery rhyme, which was born out of fortune-telling rhymes—which were born out of the most ancient of our myths—and which sends "Mother Goose goose bumps" down my spine to this day.

From the ancient Sumerian and Babylonian astrologers, the dwellers of the Mesopotamian cradle of life, to Jewish and Egyptian mystics, to the Persian, Greek, Roman, Norse, and Germanic cultures and languages, to China, Japan, and India and the four corners of the world—you name it—all of our great ancient civilizations christened the seven days of the week using the same five "naked eye" or visible planets, plus the Sun and Moon. These celestial bodies, named after their associated Gods and Goddesses, were our forebearers' Rulers or Governors, and thus, babies born on Monday contained a different set of traits and were led by a different series of "laws" than babies born on Friday.

If you want to answer the question, "Who am I?"—and who doesn't?—consult the seven days of the week.

But before diving deeper into who we are, based on the day we were born and what our future might be if we all got to know ourselves and got our act together, let's paint a fuller picture of who we once were, collectively.

Our ancient ancestors, or as I like to call them, the Ancients, looked to the heavens to answer their many mysteries. While some of their questions differed from those we ask today, we know, thanks to cave explorers and hikers bumbling across ancient petroglyphs, farmers accidentally digging up bones and artifacts in their fields, and archaeologists conducting modern-day CT scans of mummies, that the most crucial and challenging questions are eerily and eternally human. Who am I? Who are we? Why am I/are we here? What is my/our purpose?

When we roamed the Earth in tribes, following the seasons and Ra's arc from morning to night, nights were pitch black. Darkness then was deeper and thicker in virtually every corner of the globe than it is now or ever will be again. The only light pollution was the light of the stars themselves. And noise pollution, there was none. In fact, in my imagination, the Ancients could hear the stars, or at least the ones that were falling. Whizzzzzzzz, whooooosh. Why not?

This immediate proximity to the heavens above put our ancestors in direct dialogue with their planetary Rulers. If a thunderous storm prevented a small group of hunters or soldiers from being able to hold onto their weapons and use them, or if this storm sent down a bolt of lightning that caught a field they would have foraged or harvested on fire, what did the Ancients do? They spoke directly to the sky. They appeased the Gods and Goddesses with sound, music, word, dance, food, smoke, flame, or even life, in the form of a blood sacrifice. They chanted to the stars, the Sun, the Moon, the planets, developing over time a bond based on reciprocity and abundance. They revered Mother Earth, as my family did when we invested our hours, love, and energy into the land we lived on and depended on.

The Ancients erected the Colossus of Rhodes in honor of Helios, the Greek sun God. They built extensive and elaborate aqueducts to support the gardens at the "Gate of the Gods," aka Babylon. They set a statue of Zeus atop the Lighthouse of Alexandria and the statue of Zeus at Olympia was surrounded by a reflecting pool that magnified his already impressive height of forty-three feet. Wilderness and its bounty were worshipped at the Temple of Artemis, where refugees also sought safety and shelter. Larger-than-life-sized statues adorned the Mausoleum at Halicarnassus, and gigantic friezes illustrated multiple battles between Greeks and the all-female warrior tribe, the gigantic Amazons. Reconstructions of each of these nonextant wonders show they were built to reach to the Heavens, and to reach us, in one way, shape, or form.

The Great Pyramid of Giza is still standing and studied. Handling the sacred site more carefully today than researchers, visitors, and certainly thieves and pillagers have over the past centuries, scientists are using high tech tools such as gas detectors, scintillator horoscopes, and special films to reveal never-before-seen or accessed chambers, tombs, passageways, and voids. This seventh wonder has not yet revealed all its secrets, but we do know that during the Golden Age of Egypt in which it was constructed, the worship of the sun God, Ra, grew in popularity and intensity, and kings had begun to claim themselves as his direct incarnation.

Living below as the Gods and Goddesses lived above was a pursuit, or at least a dream, of some of our ancient ancestors. Learning how we might best survive and accept our journey even further below—as in six-feet under—was also a question that pressed on their minds and souls. Where were the boundaries between worlds and who made them? Who or what did we have to appease and what exactly did we have to make amends for? Who am I here and now, who will I be tomorrow, and what will become of me once I am gone?

Our Messengers, Governors, Rulers have always traveled, played, and observed and influenced us from above. We bathe in their glow, their energy, their sound, and their elements. If we pay attention and make the effort, we can engage in a dialogue with our literal higher powers, much like the Ancients did.

The quest to survive—to find food, to stay warm, to procreate, and in my mind, probably to dance and pass along stories—led to the birth of astronomy. As we began to observe and to decipher the movements of the stars, the planets, the sun, and the moon, we created our own human rhythms and calendars. We mirrored what we saw when we craned our necks to look skyward.

But because this initial growing knowledge of the physics of the universe and nature did not help us understand our place, exactly, astrology was created. Then came alchemy, which was a combination of astronomy and astrology, physics and chemistry, medicine and metallurgy, and mysticism and spirituality. During the burgeoning, blossoming, and intertwining of so much thought, belief, and science, the Ancients were taking notes. They scribbled away furiously, first on stone and then on papyrus. They built monuments they never imagined would crumble: "Dear Future Humans. Please understand this…"

By reading the symbols and words of some of the first Scribes of God, or of the great minds of the Ancient age, we keep conversations alive. We transcend the past, present, and future; we transcend the world and the afterworld. We have so much more wisdom to mine than we think we do.

As a kid, I heard echoes of the Big Bang in fireworks. I saw the Big Bang replicated in school films about the volcanoes I was surrounded by. Running my fingers over the lines of a honu's shell (a green tortoise), I knew I was touching the universe, I was, and still am, fascinated by the universe. My dreams came to me from the Time Before Time, and when I scratched out my very first short stories, I prayed to and channeled Thoth, God of the Word, God of writing, he who was said to be born from the lips of Ra.

Our Ancients built circles, cairns, and pyramids to track the sun and mark their way. They sought to know and master the climate, honor the dead, and perhaps to balance the Earth. In touch with the skies, Gods, and Goddesses in ways we no longer are, they were the original students and masters of sacred geometry. They used math, muscle, and magic to bring a single ray of light to a pile of bones buried deep within a tomb, on just one day of the year—usually on spring or winter solstice. Luckily for us, the words of the Ancients cross over.

Hermes Trismegistus said:

"That which is above is like that which is below, and that which is below is like that which is above, to achieve the wonders of the one thing. Macrocosmos is the same as microcosmos. The Universe is the same as God, God is the same as man, man is the same as the cell, the cell is the same as the atom, the atom is the same as . . . and so on, ad infinitum."

My interpretation of this statement is that God, our Creator, created us, the human race, in his image. The Macrocosm, or the Universe, is the same as the microcosm, or the universe inside the human race and inside each human being. Everything, whether visible to the naked eye, or not, is one: every quantum of energy, every cell, every atom, every human system, every human being, and every planet contains our universe and our creator. Religion is science, and vice versa. The "Atum" of the Ancients is the "Adam" of religion and the "atom" of science.

Some search "space" or the "last frontier." Some search different dimensions of the Universe and different levels of Consciousness. Some do their searching through meditation, which is sometimes called the "lost frontier," but which was also the "first and original frontier." This is the frontier that can only be found within, within the consciousness of the human being and the consciousness of the cosmic mind. This frontier, this space, is now the "lost frontier" though, because very few people are searching for answers within themselves these days. We have been taught to search the external and the exoteric world for knowledge. But no, we contain it. We only have to give it space, respect, and energy.

You are a banyan tree and a seventh wonder. So am I. I am a Friday's child and my ruling planet is beautiful Venus, but Hermes was my first favorite go-to guide. I believe we are surrounded by many modern-day mercurial messengers, ones we can learn from in order to live better lives, fulfill our purpose, and save ourselves and our place, our planet. Ancient Hermes soul and essence lives amongst us today. He is part God, part Goddess, and part us. We are all part Maui, part Hermes, part every God and Goddess that ever hovered over us and fell to us. The Gods and the Goddesses could not resist us; they mingled and tingled with the Ancients, and here we are today—demigods and demigoddesses.

Hermes, a lucky trickster and a monkey-around'er'er, carried to us the Caduceus. The intertwining snakes represent, amongst many things, reciprocity and the interchange of ideas and energy. With the touch of his staff, the dead could be brought back to life, and the living could be granted a gentle death. Perhaps it is because of this life and death association that hospitals and doctors have mistakenly used the Caduceus as their logo.

If Hermes were to enter a hospital today, he would be shocked to see the tool of his trade(s) being so literally associated with medicine and healthcare. It is Asclepius, the god of healing and medicine, whose rod—a branch with a single snake wrapped around it—should be emblazoned on medical signage everywhere. But it isn't. Of all the messages Hermes has delivered, some have not been correctly interpreted — most importantly how this symbol, his staff, is a representation of how we are created with the fingerprint of the universe and the DNA of the planets.

Hermes lives on at 777 Giza Boulevard, and yes, there is a McDonald's nearby and the light pollution from its arches annoys him. But because he is a God, he understands that "it is what it is" better than most of us do. Hermes reads his paper, *The Pyramid Times,* with his dog, Sphinx, at his feet. In his Facebook profile, he describes himself as a God, a Son of God, a Master, A Saint, a King, a High Priest, or the human race's inheritance from Atlantis. He notes that he inspired the earliest civilizations by inventing science, medicine, philosophy, music, art, language, and writing. He majored in astronomy, astrology, and alchemy—the triple A's of the question "Who am I?"

He is not known for being humble, but what God is?

He is known for building the pyramids, one of which graces the back of the most circulated papyrus of our day, the dollar bill. He has taught many of my muses, from Abraham and Moses, to Pythagoras and Socrates, to Paracelsus and Sir Isaac Newton, to Albert Einstein and Rudolph Steiner. Friends call him "He who cannot lose to a computer in a game of chess."

He sometimes feels remorseful for having invented the Seven Day Week, which led to the first reported case of "the Mondays." He generally resists TV, but if he made a guest appearance on Sesame Street, it would have been on July 7th, 1977, and that episode would have been brought to you by the letter "Y" and the number "7."

Hermes rejects tabloids and Planet Hollywood. His stars are the stars of our universe.

CHAPTER FIVE

THE OLD AGE AND THE POWER OF SEVEN

I WILL ALWAYS BE A CHILD OF THE ISLANDS AND WILL ALWAYS BELIEVE IN Time Before Time and the stories that originated there. Myth is as much a part of me as Maui, and my senses will always be attuned to the roots of the tree I am sitting under as much as they are to the branches above me, reaching skyward. I'm a history buff and a mystery lover. I'm a fan of superbeings with magical powers, and of thinkers with ahead-of-their-time or beyond-their-time thoughts.

Galileo Galilei spent the last decade or so of his life under house arrest. His life story is one of my favorites.

Galileo, in the book he published in 1632, *Dialogue Concerning the Two Chief World Systems*, had dared to question—and disprove—the prevailing Ptolemaic theory, that the Earth was the center of our solar system. He was tried for and accused of "heresy" for his writings, for his insistence, for his knowledge.

A medical student turned mathematician, Galileo could not resist following through on insights he gained using his keen powers of observation. He changed majors as a young man, despite what his father wanted and the fact he would make less money, after taking one geometry class. In my mind, he was a numbers and movement tracker at heart. It's said that one day, at university, he noticed a chandelier swinging in sync with the beat of his heart and went home to build pendulums to study. You cannot make up such poetic genius!

Later, pioneering the use of the telescope and studying astrology—which back in his time was linked with astronomy and math—he became fascinated by the tides. Far from my favorite waters off Maui, there he was in Venice, thinking, "How can this sea move in this way, rapidly and regularly. What is the ruling force unseen? And why?"

For all the times I've asked myself "Who am I?" I picture Galileo, with the insatiable curiosity of a two-year old, asking "Why, why, why?" about everything under, beyond, or on the sun. By the way, the Church also hated him for talking about sunspots and his tide theories were not quite accurate; but, he literally put into motion so much of what we know to be true today about our universe. He stood up to Tycho Brahe and the Tychonic System, in which the five naked-eye planets revolved around the sun, while the Sun, the Moon, and stars revolved around the Earth.

Brahe is another favorite seeker scientist of mine, because he was looking to solve great mysteries of the heavens with the technology of his era, mainly the sextant and the quadrant. Brahe is known as one of the last "naked-eye" planet astronomers, and despite missing out, for the most part, on the use of the telescope to observe astronomical phenomena, he is known for his beyond-average powers of observation. One American astronomer and historian, Dennis Rawlins, wrote about one of Tycho's famous star catalogs in an article for *The International Journal of Scientific History*, stating: "In it, Tycho achieved, on a mass scale, a precision far beyond that of earlier catalogers. Cat D represents an unprecedented confluence of skills: instrumental, observational, & computational—all of which combined to enable Tycho to place most of his hundreds of recorded stars to an accuracy of ordermag 1!"

Lingo such as "ordermag" is Greek to me—or maybe even Geek to me—but it does not prevent me from being in awe of our earliest scientists' pursuit of answers. I am dazzled by what they were able to see with the naked eye, and I dream of the starry skies they knew, especially when I am visiting any large city and the light pollution interferes with my sense of connection to the celestial bodies I am derived from.

Tycho sketched his stars, all while holding respect for religion. His model of the universe was part geocentric for this reason: "All the earth is at peace and at rest, Isaiah 14:7." Yes, he believed the Earth was too heavy to rotate around the Sun.

He believed astrology was valid and wrote horoscopes in his earlier years. This practice, of course, was common at the time. Mathematicians and astronomers/astrologers looked to the skies to help royals predict not just meteorological events, but wars, floods, and betrayals. Tycho was his own brand of rebel—he believed the practice of observation was more crucial than pure logic and reason when it came to solving the many mysteries of how and why things work. Born in a castle, he never gave a damn about what others thought of him or his methods. It is said he turned away from his study of law in 1563, after witnessing the conjunction of Saturn and Jupiter.

And some people believe the planets do not hold power over the course of their life?

Brahe said, "Those who study the stars have God for a teacher."

Whatever our religion or spiritual bent, when things are going wrong or we are seeking special council or inspiration, we raise our eyes to the heavens. When we celebrate a new marriage or a birthday, we toss birdseed or song into the air. We set off fireworks to celebrate freedom, or a way of life. Me, I picture Zeus and Hera up there lounging on the clouds, enjoying the attention, enjoying the communion, enjoying the show. They must be proud of old Galileo, Tycho, and Tycho's assistant, Johannes Kepler. They must know we still have a lot to learn. They watch over us, and they—or some God—sends angels down to walk amongst us.

Angels, I believe, were present on the day the Earth was created—however it was created. And angels, or archangels, though their names differ across mythologies, religions, and stories, guide us. They work between us, the heavens, and the Gods and Goddesses—the very word angel is rooted in the Latin word angelus, meaning "messenger."

As I am part Maui and part Hermes, Hermes is part angel.

And though in some churches there are seven angels and in others three, or one, angels, like the planets, are our Watchers.

Michael, Gabriel, Camael, Raphael, Sachiel, Anael, and Cassiel—the seven angels (or Archangels) for the seven days of the week. Whether we believe we can see them or not, they do, as they have done since the dawn of time, the divine work of maintaining a gentle order.

Gabriel informed Mary she would give birth to Jesus.

After Jesus's first encounter with Satan, angels came by to pat him on the back—"Good job passing *that* test!"

Angels had Jesus' back through and after his death, alerting Mary and others that he had risen.

Sure, it is true that between the 16th and 17th centuries, the rise of logic and reason widened chasms between philosophers, scientists, and the church. Thinkers and doers in each field fought amongst themselves as well. The explosion, or the blossoming of intellectual, social, political, cultural, and artistic ideas, naturally led to chaos, confusion, sometimes war, and often, peace, clarity, and rebirth. From tumult, came invention, innovation, and inspiration.

Hawaii was born thanks to Maui and his magical fishing hook, and it is continually reborn thanks to Pele and her volcanoes. Pele eats the Earth to create Earth. It takes a village—of Gods and Goddesses, angels, planets, stars, and humans—to maintain a healthy balance, a functioning system of checks and balances, a perpetual sense of forward motion and wonder.

When Galileo and his peers began using the telescope to view the stars, around 1609 or 1610, what did they feel? We read their notes and study their meticulous diagrams, but between those lines and circles, I see a bunch of scientists jumping up and down with raw joy in their hearts.

They were the pioneers awe and of As Above, so below. They are our Messengers, our Record Keepers. Their quest forms and informs the center of our universe, the center of our spirit.

What these astrologer-astronomer-mathematicians had only been able to observe mainly as specks of light—or, in the case of comets, as specks of light with tails—they could now see magnified, three to four times closer. Fiddling with the glass of the concave and convex lenses over time, Galileo and his peers eventually improved the devices so that they could magnify an object ten, then twenty, then thirty times over. Determined to see more than a sliver of the full Moon at one time, or to verify, for once and for all what held the center of our universe—the Earth or the Sun—these great thinkers forged an entire industry of telescope manufacturing!

With his twenty-three-foot long telescope, in 1659, Christiaan Huygens viewed Orion. He wrote that the stars in Orion's sword created the effect of "an opening in the sky through which a brighter region was visible."

There is always more than the naked eye can see. There is infinitely more than today's most powerful telescopes can see. And what about microscopes? What we see in the sky, we see in the lab. The Fibonacci spiral is seen in a crosscut of an ovary of an Anglerfish and in the way cancer cells divide. Fibonacci is in our fingerprints. As Above, so below.

With improvements in telescopes, we learned that our Moon played a role in the Earth's tides. We have since learned that when the full moon rises, our local law enforcement authorities go on higher alert than usual. Our Moon pulls our inner tides and waters. We are 99% water, so how could we even doubt we all feel a little extra loony when the lunar cycle reaches its maximum capacity?

By around 800 B.C., the Chinese knew that the Sun had sunspots. They simply could see them with the naked eye, and they believed reading these spots helped them predict the future. Galileo and his peers, peering through their telescopes, thought sunspots were clouds or shadows. They tracked them as well as they could to help figure out the length of the Sun's rotation period. Little did they know these eye-like, sunflower-like imperfections on the surface of our great ball of fire would one day "interfere" with modern technology. Solar flares and solar ejections (known as coronal mass ejections) are just as powerful as Mercury Retrograde, in terms of their capacity to cause disruption in communications and in our electromagnetic field.

Galileo—he never stopped looking. I can picture him squinting so hard he'd almost burst a blood vessel trying to figure out what he was seeing around Saturn. He is credited with discovering Saturn's rings, but he did not call them rings at the time. Through his crude lenses, he believed he was looking at two moons, which he later labeled "arms." Huygens, also an insatiable sky explorer, correctly declared Saturn had rings. He was also the first to discover one of Saturn's many actual moons.

The Martian Problem was solved by Brahe's assistant, Kepler. What he boasted he would solve in a week, took years, but thanks to his obsession, he did it. Kepler discovered that Mars orbited the Sun at a much slower pace than Earth did, which was why Mars appeared to move backwards in the sky. Kepler figured out the further a planet from the sun, the slower it moved.

Mercury, of course, Hermes' planet and my personal favorite, was a speed demon. And it was Galileo's discovery of the phases of Venus, which helped undermine the prevailing theory that the Earth was the center of the universe, which peeved the Church the most.

Galileo, for a spell, studied the use of light and shadow in art. Did the sunspots he mistook for clouds and shadows fuel his interest in chiaroscuro, or did his study of rendering artistic subjects more three-dimensional influence the way he could see? He studied so many topics, that even if we followed a strict timeline of his passions and findings, we would still only be guessing at which came first—the chicken or the egg (the egg, by the way, contains another Fibonacci spiral).

Galileo was the first to see mountains and craters on the moon, and these discoveries would influence the way artists then approached one of the most popular subjects of the time: The Virgin Mary. When Galileo wrote to his painter friend, Cigoli about what he found, Cigoli leapt onto the heretic train! In part of a mural he was commissioned to paint on the dome of the Pauline Chapel in Rome, he painted the *Assumption of the Virgin*. This representation contrasts with earlier paintings in which all Moon/Virgin associations were "immaculate" in nature. Knowing the Moon was "maculata," or covered in spots, and not as purely smooth and white as was previously imagined, the Moon could no longer be a direct symbol of Mary.

We cannot leave Italy and art without retrograding in time and taking a look at Michelangelo's *The Last Judgment*. In this masterpiece of flesh and sky, is Christ illuminating the seven deadly sins? Is he rotating his arms in reference and reverence to the Heavens and the Heavenly cycles? Do we see the seven virtues represented? Yes, to all of the above. Yes, I see hope, charity, faith, justice, temperance, fortitude, courage and prudence set in light of each of its darker counterparts.

I see that as our ancestors were attempting to put the pieces—visible and invisible—together, they fed off one another's inspiration. They used one another's tools—Galileo was an illustrator, a mathematician, and so on. Cigoli was a painter who sought to stay true to science. Kings relied on scientists to tell them what their Watchers, their Gods and Goddesses, expected of them, and held in store for them.

Was there turmoil? Were there plagues? Were the Gods and Goddesses to forever battle demons, trick one another, cast one another aside? Would we mortal humans always seek to appease them?

Yes, to all of the above.

And as time marches forward as it does, in a spiral, let's not lose sight of the words of Tycho Brahe: "It is important to know that the seven planets in the heavens correspond to the seven metals on earth and the seven most important organs in man. All these things have been so finely and harmonically arranged in relation to each other, that they seemed almost to have the same function, type and nature."

As Above, so below. As in Heaven, so on Earth.

CHAPTER SIX

THE CONTEMPORARY AGE
AND THE POWER OF SEVEN

T HE HEAD INJURY I SUFFERED AFTER FALLING OFF THE BACK OF MY parents' Jeep in Hana was not my last. I was a quiet kid—an observer, a Watcher—but all my life I've been an outdoors adventurer. Whether climbing trees, meditating on a mountain ridge, skiing mountains, or playing in the surf, I have always engaged with the beauty of this planet I was born to. Mother Earth gives me caves to slither down into and volcanic trails to hike and bike, and I'm grateful. I believe my injuries—fractures, scrapes, and scuffs—have actually gifted me, by nudging my already curious nature further still.

Like so many mystery-lover-explorers, I learned about Joseph Campbell and *The Power of Myth* and *The Hero With a Thousand Faces* in my late teens and early twenties. Campbell, who died the day before Halloween in 1987, on Oahu, Hawaii, is a mythological figure in his own right. An avid researcher of history, anthropology, religion, philosophy, and psychology, when people talk about "finding their bliss," they are channeling Campbell, who developed his notions on bliss and how to achieve transcendence, while reading the Upanishads. Now there's a resource for insights that help answer that question, "Who am I?"

A great fan of Carl Jung and the interpretation of dreams, Campbell was a consummate decipherer of symbols. He believed that in a bullfight, the matador in his brilliant uniform represented the Sun, and the bull, in his hovering massiveness, the Moon. This battle between them was a way of maintaining balance and establishing who was primary. The Sun needed to kill the Moon in order to shine the next day. Marriage was a similar battle: in Campbell's mind saying, "I do" to another entailed the "killing" of the self as a separate entity. Some of his ideas, of course, were controversial.

And some of his ideas are completely ingrained in our consciousness.

Myth, for Campbell, was a way of storytelling, a way for humans to find the meaning of, and the meaning in their own existence. When I picture our first ancestors looking to the Heavens and recording how they believed the Gods, Goddesses, planets, and stars were all linked to them, I see them recording a message that would transcend all time. Stars and planets are time; stars and planets are messages, or story, in constant motion. Our ancestors were what they saw and "invented" through symbols and words (which are symbols). With the Word, what our ancestors said and recorded about what they saw, mirrored and reinforced who they were. Our ancestors are us, and we are them. As Above, so below—eternally.

Campbell's gathering of tales from around the world and his notion of the "monomyth," stem, in my mind, from the first question and the first Word. Essentially, common desires, needs, and beliefs all sprout from one seed, which impacts all storytelling today. The archetypical hero, before fully stepping into their title and role as hero, is called from their routine, mundane, or ordinary existence to sacrifice, battle, and survive what most of us "regular folks" would consider near-impossible conditions, challenges, and events. Meeting archetypical teachers, enemies, and allies along the way, this hero-in-the-making transforms, ultimately returning to where they came from with a gift.

The hero's journey reverberates through hundreds of short stories and novels we read today. Campbell's notions of the monomyth (he borrowed the term from James Joyce) have informed some of the top Hollywood screenwriters and producers or our time. *Indiana Jones*, the *Matrix*, and *Star Wars IV, V, and VI* are all films directly or indirectly seen as influenced by Joseph Campbell, or as George Lucas called him, "Joe."

So what if Hermes—one of my lifelong heroes—were to audition for a role in *Star Wars*? I think he would try out for and be cast as a droid, an R2D2 or a C3PO. The way I see it, the droids in *Star Wars*, like all seven of the major characters, represent one of the seven planets and Seven Planetary Archetypes—they are the Sidereal Seven. R2D2 and C3PO are Mercury, the God of communication, languages, science, technology, computers, logic, ration, and reason (they are Hermes). Obi Wan Kenobi is the Moon, the master of the mind, the mystic and the visionary. Princess Leia is beautiful Venus, the Goddess of love, beauty, the arts, balance, diplomacy, and peace. Han Solo, the arrogant leader, is the Sun, the God of kings, leaders, aspirations, confidence, and self-centeredness. Luke Skywalker, the warrior and hero, is Mars, the God of battles, competition, winning, anger, and hate. Yoda, masters, higher values and morals is!

And Darth Vader is Saturn, the God of death, decay, and darkness.

What connects them all throughout the *Star Wars* space opera is an invisible energy, or "the Force." This "verse" of the "universe" is a mantra and it is spoken and repeated throughout the decades: "Luke, the Force will be with you," Obi-Wan Kenobi says in the original *Star Wars* film.

"May the Force be with you," Leia, now Commander Organa, tells Rey, in the final line of *The Force Awakens*.

The Force is continually referred to and it is what these characters—our heroes—must continually tap into if they are to keep light shining in the face of darkness. The struggle to discover and maintain one's identity, to find one's way through the universe, and to fulfill one's soul is eternal. The motifs illustrated by Joseph Campbell's analysis of a bullfight or of marriage roll on.

Time too rolls on. The Sun and the Moon tumble day in and day out for dominance, but in truth, they exist equally as they dance. When the Moon takes over in San Francisco, the Sun is waking people up in Paris. Sunday turns to Monday, and we cycle through another seven days. We make our plans while simultaneously tapping into the realm of the Gods and Goddesses and their Seven Planetary Archetypes.

We cannot forget that one in seven of us is born on a Sunday, and we are like Han Solo—or "sol," the Sun; or "solo," the one at the center. We are the noble leader, the authoritative light, and the ego. When we first meet Han, he is looking for his fare, his business, his treasure and his gold. Later, we learn he has a warm, compassionate heart.

One in seven of us are born on a Monday. We are like Obi Wan, and like the Moon. We are the protector, the reflector and the Zen Master of feelings and intuition and though we dwell sometimes in a cave, or in the darkness of the subconscious, at the same we can and do travel as a vision and as a visionary, especially in times of need or urgency.

Born on a Tuesday, one out of every seven of us is like Luke Skywalker, or Mars. The skilled warrior with his sword, or lightsaber, the athlete, we train in order to master the duality of nature. In gaining the skills to tame what is dark in us, we tame what is dark in our ancestors (our Father) and the universe.

One in seven of us—born on Wednesday—are like the droids, R2D2 and C3PO, and like Mercury. We are consciousness of science, technology, ration, reason, communication, languages, transport, intelligence and intellect. When all around is at risk of drowning in a flood of emotion, we cut to the chase and proceed in a way that will help save the day.

Those of us born on Thursday are Yoda. (Don't worry, we are all a little Yoda, because we are a little of everything!) Like Jupiter, we are gurus and teachers, sages and seers. We are all-knowing. We are the green forest dwellers and judicial philanthropists. We are the holy wearing robes.

Born on Friday, we are like Princess Leia and Venus. Beauty abounds in, around, and for us. Peace is possible, and kindness too. In her youth, Leia is the lover or the desired feminine. Luke and Han fight over her for affection and attention. Through Leia's diplomacy and Words—she says, "I love you" to Han—harmony is achieved and light is restored.

Saturday babies, like Saturn and Darth Vader, convey seriousness, control and order. They hold the darkness that is normal and necessary for life, and that contrasts with light. Darth Vader, with his Death Star and death grip, is a monster to be feared, until we learn his backstory.

Darth Vader's story though, is our story.

Saturn has its dark side, but because it rotates on an axis, its light side exists too, in equal measure. Each of the seven planets and Seven Planetary Archetypes presents a dual nature. Luke, the handsome good guy, was Darth Vader's son, and so he carried anger, aggression, and the desire for revenge within him. His conquering of this darkness was necessary in order for him to save the day. One of the "takeaway gifts" of his hero's journey was his learning from a trusted mentor to soothe his own mind and nature, and to make progress via balance.

Within the seven-fold pattern of the universe, Hermes understood that this Yin and the Yang were present in every living thing. He communicated for others and between others, but he also put our inner halves (light and dark, rational and emotional, scientific and sensual—you name it), in touch so that we could attain wholeness. We do not have to fully reject or kill one element of our nature in order for the other elements to shine and thrive; in fact, we must embrace the fact we are living and breathing contradictions. We are Han Solo, Obi Wan Kenobi, Luke Skywalker, R2D2 or C3PO, Yoda, Princess Leia, and Darth Vader—all in one, all one!

Look at the amazing journey each of those characters has taken in the forty-plus years in which we have watched their myths unfold.

Hermes knew that the "truth" was "one." He stood for this truth, and for communicating it. He lived before our first and original wisdom expanded not only throughout the minds of the human race, but also throughout the world and the universe. Fortunately, Hermes was a great teacher and would not allow our wisdom, and all its mysteries to lose its "force" as it still impacts our psyche today.

When we sit in the movie theater and watch those words scroll from some unseen place in space right before our eyes, when we watch those words receding into the distance and being swallowed by stars, we are reading Cosmic Law, or the "old astrology." The *Star Wars* myth—with all of its clas-sical archetypes, motifs, and symbols—reaches across continents and nations, languages and cultures, and genres and generations. Who knows, maybe the funny May 4th Meme "May the Fourth Be With You," has reached other life forms in other universes, and they know we have a sense of humor. What we do know is that on an unconscious level, *Star Wars* resides in all of us, and the Force is with us.

Joseph Campbell said that stories "speak to something inside us that wants to know how our world lives, that wants to make order of it and find some meaning. Myths fulfill that in a way that science and facts don't always do, because science and facts don't always give us meaning."

The mysteries I have always been drawn to are a mix of story, myth, history, art, spirituality, and science. I appreciate the fact that no single human, no single religion, and no single branch of the arts and sciences holds the answers to it all. Just as each of us embodies elements of each of the Seven Planetary Archetypes, each of us is attempting to construct the puzzle of reality in our own way. *Who am I?* is a complex process, which is why sitting under a tree and lifting one's eyes to the Heavens helps. We are continually putting pieces of ourselves together As Above, so below, from the time of Zeus and the Parthenon to the time of Stephen Hawking and the rebuilding of the Notre Dame cathedral.

If the one key to the universe were offered to me, I'm not sure I would take it. My mother's teacher, held some of the keys to part of the universe. When I was a young boy watching him teach her, I could almost see the wisdom emanating from his skin. His Yoda-ness rubbed off on me enough that I eventually became his student too. But never was there any request from me or any promise from him that I would eventually "know" everything I wanted to know. Always, the message was that "the Force" (I am using the term, he didn't) existed in the desire to be open-minded and openhearted, and to be brave in my quest to always observe, question, and learn more.

When I first sat down on 7/7/7 to put together my observations, questions, and discoveries, I had no idea the words I was committing to the page would begin to write me. I had no idea the words would begin to take the shape of a book, and that the book that was originating from my own flow of wondering would humble me and yet keep me hungry.

I am no hero, but I am on a transformative journey—a journey that began with the number seven. In reading the words of others, I seek out the right words and I put them in an order that makes sense to me, an order that thrills me. I use the Word and am written by the Word, so that in some ancient-to-today variation of the monomyth, I can carry forward a way of figuring out what it all means to be alive on this planet, in this solar system, in this galaxy.

The mentors and guides I have had during my time on this planet echo those who have led me from way beyond their graves. The teachers of my Waldorf School years in Hawaii were part of my evolution. Inspired themselves, by Rudolf Steiner, a forefather of modern organic farming, art therapy, and mantric verse, each year—from kindergarten through seventh grade—they moved up grade-by-grade with my class. These teachers knew me. They knew I wanted to sit at the back of the schoolroom and listen, observe, and remain unseen. They gave me extra support when my time came to stand in front of the class and speak—from my show-and-tell years through to those dreaded oral reports.

At the end of each school year, they watched over me, over all of us, as we made our own candles, and then constructed our own candleholders out of clay. At the end of each year, they escorted us—this small group of students they were getting to know through time—to the spiral. Every year, we walked the spiral, our single candle in hand, with the notion of bringing light to the darkness and to merging our flame with the big flame at the center.

One year, I made a candleholder in the form of a serpent. Was I aware at that age that I was designing a spiral to carry through a spiral? Was a snake just a snake to me then, or was part of me, through the teachings of Waldorf and all my adventures on Maui attuned to a higher symbolism? I don't know, but I do know, myth was as stamped into my DNA as was the color of my eyes.

The Ancients believed that the sun revolved around a flat earth. They believed sky Gods and Goddesses controlled the weather, the seasons, and the tides. Nowadays, a majority of people believe that myths are just that—*myths*. But I believe that we are the myths, the legends, and the folklore of our ancient past. We are history—past, present, and future—living and reliving the same stories over and over again.

Each of us is one of the Seven Planetary Archetypes and once we re-learn to understand all the original knowledge and wisdom contained in these archetypes, we will again be able to understand our first and original language—the language of God, of our Creator. Reconnecting with the laws and cycles of creation, we will be able to answer the first and original questions: Who am I? What is the human race? What is the universe? The language of Symbol will reappear, and give us access to Olympus, and to what Campbell called the "secret opening of the cosmos," and the "mythological age" and understand how "in our inner organism we have an image of the entire cosmos."

CHAPTER SEVEN

TIME AND WHERE WE FIT
IN THE SEVEN DAYS OF THE WEEK

TIME IS RELATIVE—WE DON'T NEED TO BE PHYSICISTS OR ASTRONOMERS to understand that. Anyone who has waited in line to eat at their favorite restaurant or to see their favorite band understands that the time we spend in that line passes quickly or slowly in part, depending on who we are waiting with. Anyone who has grieved the loss of a friend or loved one knows that time warps and is punctured and pacified in ways that are almost alien to our daily human experience.

If you have spent any time in the Twilight Zone, either coming out of surgery or experimenting with psychotropics, you might understand time as a game or a matrix. You might have seen yourself from the point of view of the you of parallel time.

Twilight, since the dawn of time, has been considered the span of morning and evening where the membrane that divides the material and the spiritual world is at its most tenuous. Fires are lit, prayers are chanted, spaces are smudged at twilight—much as they are during the summer and winter solstices, and during the spring and fall equinoxes.

Time, like the division of the sacred and the mundane, is an illusion. It is a system the Ancients created long ago, based on their observations of the Sun, the Moon, and the naked eye planets. We hunted, fished, and harvested according to seasons and tides, which the animals instinctually followed. Time is astronomy, or an astronomer. It's no wonder, with my celestial obsession, that I spend so much time thinking about time.

Time is math, and because of that, it is comforting. I don't always want to wake up when my alarm sounds and I am not a fan of how pressed for time many of us feel throughout our work week, but I can count on time to help keep me focused and dependable. Our Watchers above—our ruling planets with their Gods and Goddesses—have us covered non-stop, 24/7; so, we can turn our devices off once in a while, leave our watches in a desk drawer, and relax. We all have the power to *free time* by setting time aside!

I subscribe to the very ancient and very popular Contemporary pop culture mantra "Be present," but I also, obviously, like to ponder the past. I don't live in the past, but I know the past lives in me. We die, but time and all it absorbs never dies. Our physical bodies come and go, but our essence is eternally recycled. If you track the Sun from the same spot every day over the course of the year, taking a photo of it at the same time of day, the result is an analemma—a diagram that resembles the sign for infinity. We are all analemmas; we are infinite.

In the infinite Time Before Time I believe in, I refer to all that existed and took place before recorded history as we have *traditionally* defined it. I have dreams about this age, and the primary image that comes to me when I've got my eyes closed—or when I am otherwise calm and paying attention—is a Great Spiral City. We once walked from the periphery of this Time Before Time city, or place, to the center, either by slowly circling inward on a land-based path, as I did as a child attending the Waldorf School on Maui; or, we would cross a strip of land, then water, land then water, alternating this way when taking a short cut.

However one traversed this Great Spiral in the Time Before Time, in my visions of it, I experience a powerful deju vu—"I know this place,"—and a simultaneous, "Where the hell am I?" The place is familiar and unknown. Its two most prominent features, set in the center of the spiral, are a Great Pyramid and a Great Statue. These features look similar to the Great Pyramid of Giza and the Sphinx, but they are a much earlier version—a version that has somehow been entirely preserved.

The Great Pyramid of my dreamtime—or as Hermes Instagramming about this era might write, *#TB4T*—is larger than any structures that exist on Earth today. Its capstone is so brilliant that nobody can look at it directly. The material the capstone is made of is unfamiliar. It is diamond or crystal-like, but it is metal—an ancient metal belonging exclusively to the alchemists of the time. The peak of this pyramid illuminates the landscape by reflecting and refracting the light of the universe. As Above, so below . . . the stars and the planets shine directly above, onto, and through the inhabitants of this pristine and peaceful place.

From the capstone too, comes the "Sound" that we in the contemporary world no longer hear with our ears. This is the Sound too many of us have forgotten to listen for. But I know this sound—it is the Hum of the Universe, the Word or the Big Bang. It is the sound that is so old and ancient, that it will appear to be new, yet at the same time will seem so, so familiar, as if we have heard it all along. It is the sound within silence and the sound between notes. Unlike the thunder without which prognosticates the lightning without, it is the Light within which prognosticates the Sound within. It is the Sound of Light! It is what we sense when we meditate.

The Time Before Time statue that I initially recognize as a Sphinx is much larger that the Sphinx of our time. It glimmers with an armor of white light and stands guard, or acts as Watcher over all Riddles and Mysteries. It differs from the great creature hundreds of thousands of tourists flock to in Egypt every year in another way too: the building it reposes on houses a great library. In the library are the texts of Time Before Time—pages of hidden and forgotten wisdom, codes, and secrets.

I'm not sure whether to call my Time Before Time place Atlantis Revised or Revisited, as it is not entirely Atlantean. All I know is that once upon a time, the Earth was different. Knowledge and wisdom reigned and were accessible to every living soul, in equal measure, as if the Library of Alexandria remained with all of its books and gnosis intact to be shared with future generations. Long before my friend Galileo improved upon the utilization of the telescope, science, astronomy, and mathematics were flourishing. Ages before Luciano Pavarotti belted out "Nessum Dorma" (*none shall sleep*), song existed and everyone had a voice in the choir. The Word mattered and the Number did too. Nature was primary.

When I think of modern Egypt, I think of a typical metropolis bursting with millions of people. Traffic runs day and night, sidewalks swarm with business people and vacationers, children kick a soccer ball back and forth in a park and old men play chess there. This bustling city is nestled in next to a lost, hidden, and forgotten world. Camels, ancient-looking beasts that they are, roam in parts of the city and on its outskirts. And in some strange way, these camels see, they hear, they know, of the hidden city I dream of. This twilight-infused place of my Time Before Time reverie is a world so different than that of camels and King Tut, but it is the singular universe we all ascended from, and so it is ours to revisit.

Our original home is a lush, tropical garden with a great river spiraling through it. Expanding outward from the central Great Pyramid is a colossal city, a city of concentric rings where energy moves like the ripples on a pond's surface after a stone has been plunked into it. This city is nestled in the most circular portion of the spiral, but with its surroundings, in totality, it forms the perfect Fibonacci spiral.

This Great Spiral functions flawlessly, harmoniously, and with purpose, like a humming atom. Each ring of the city is at a distance that equals the space between the planets of our solar system and that matches the distance of intervals between our musical scales. This city is a reflection of the "As Above;" it is the mirror of a greater divine reality. It is a place we can access by putting ourselves in the right place, in the right time, and in the right frame of mind.

The Great Pyramid at the center of the Great Spiral is an "energy station:" it provides free energy and electricity to all of its inhabitants, and because they are free of incurring any sort of debt for this basic need, they themselves have more energy to share and expend. This is a city, like New York City only in that it never rests. But it is also a city of rest. The perfect geometry of it, like time and all mathematics, exudes calm and elicits confidence.

The entire place is a vortex and the only currency exchanged is energy. Creation never stops, and slowing down—or taking time to smell the roses or to sit beneath a tree and meditate—is encouraged, because there is an abundance of everything, including time.

This ancient power—which is electrifying and soothing—can be accessed and known through meditation. We unearth and learn what secrets the Great Sphinx here sits on by being archaeologists of the mind. We engage with and build a relationship with the universe by listening closely for the Sound, by reading the Word, and by looking for symbols of how As Above is playing out here, so below.

The symbols we want to draw into our consciousness are etched in my dreamscape upon the Seven Obelisks, which stand like Watchers at the perimeter of the Great Pyramid of Time Before Time. These symbols are:

From these symbols of the Sun, the Moon, and the original naked eye planets, we can trace our "folklore," or what I think of as the Word as it was originally delivered to Human Beings, by way of the Heavens.

Sitting in the Time Before Time with my back against the obelisk that is etched with the symbol of Friday, my birth day, ♀, I look to the sky and see a Seven Star Evening. It is twilight, so I see the Sun, the Moon, Mercury and Venus. I watch Mars, Jupiter, and Saturn all rise. I think of these three latecomers as long-distance runners at the start of a very long desert race, but I know each of the celestial bodies is a wanderer, a Watcher. Sitting here, I can imagine what it was like to be a pioneer of thought, to be the first human to look up at the full moon and wonder, and try to comprehend, what *it* is, what we are, who I am. Here, I realize how Pythagoras brought to us the Music of the Spheres and the correlation of the movement of the planets and music, a secret code of the universe, our destinies encoded with a rhyme and a reason. Sitting here, I can see how Hermes brought to us the Caduceus, the seven interconnecting DNA double helixes representing the seven planets and our seven vortexes, activating our seven major and seven minor organs and organ systems, tiny microscopic universes within us – as within, So Without. I wonder what happened to the Mystics and mysteries and the Sages and secrets. And I wonder what happened to our ancient Knowledge, Wisdom and Gnosis. I bow my head then in reverence, shut my eyes, and listen for the Hum so that I might be guided more gracefully along my path and toward my fate.

In the Time Before Time, when the number Seven was at the center of the universe, our Mother Culture was ceaselessly creating. Perhaps this is when "the original" Mother Goose—the goose before the goose—planted the seeds that would become the famous nursery rhyme, "Monday's Child."

> Monday's child is fair of face
> Tuesday's child is full of grace
> Wednesday's child is full of woe
> Thursday's child has far to go,
> Friday's child is loving and giving,
> Saturday's child works hard for a living,
> And the child that is born on the Sabbath day
> Is bonny and blithe, and good and gay.

When I first heard this "ditty" as a boy, I got goosebumps. I could not get it out of my head. I didn't know then that this sort of rhyme originated as a "fortune telling" rhyme, I only knew it spoke to me.

As time went on though, I realized "Monday's Child" had become part of me for a reason. Far beyond being catchy, the words were part of the Word of the universe. They traveled across space and time, telling attentive listeners—me!—about the effects space and time have on us from the moment we are born. *Friday's child is loving and giving* helped answer the question I have always had, "Who am I?"

When I was a boy, on Maui, I knew instinctively that overworking and overstressing was not part of who I was. In the classroom, I was measured, in control, and when not rebelling, rational. I was a rough and tumble kid when it came to sports, and I had the injuries, bumps, and bruises to show for it. But I was also loving and giving—a kind child that got along with others and treated them well. I was, and still am, the peacekeeper, the diplomat, the harmonious one.

Growing up on island time was a blessing. Island time was its own form of bliss, and all other concepts of time were for mainlanders. We all knew if the surf was up, the rest could wait. We knew to prioritize being one with the water, or with the land.

Beneath the banyan tree of Lahaina, the tree of my Hawaiian childhood to this day, I am present—but I am also highly aware of its history and offerings.

The majestic Lahaina banyan tree was gifted to the sheriff of Lahaina in the late 1800s. When planted, it stood eight-feet tall. Now, it reaches sixty-feet into the sky and covers a circumference of a quarter-mile. Perhaps this tree, supposedly one of the largest in the United States, is a descendent of the "Great Banyan Tree," or the "wish fulfilling tree," located in the Acharya Jagadish Chandra Bose Indian Botanic Garden, in India.

I have been coming to this tree since I was a child, and I have made a wish beneath it every single time. I am this tree; this tree is me—but oddly, as I grow older, the tree does not appear to age, or change. Does it see me growing? When I sit in its shade, my back to its trunk, does it recognize me? Does it see the wrinkles, or the rings around my eyes that were not there when I was a boy child? Does it notice that my childhood ringlets no longer fall below my shoulders and beaded necklace?

Fortunately, we know the approximate age of this banyan, and do not have to cut it to count its rings. This banyan is already suffering from draught, city development, and the continual foot traffic beneath it. This tree has seen what I have seen in Hawaii over the past forty years (and so much more)—rapid and sometimes greedy growth.

To attend to the concern I have for the land, the ocean, and the skies that I worship, I come to this tree early in the morning before most of Lahaina arises, and I take a deep breath. As my lungs fill with air, I am reminded of how are lungs look, or are, mirror images of a tree. It is twilight, so I look up to the cosmos. "Twinkle, Twinkle Little Star" vibrates in my solar plexus, and I make a wish. "Monday's Child, Friday's Child" shows up too, and I honor the dual upside-down nature of this Tree of Good and Evil, this Tree of Longevity and Immortality. This is my mythical World Tree, rooted in Heaven, the stars, the planets, the Gods and the Goddesses—with its trunk and branches planted firmly in the Earth, As Above, so below.

PART II

THE SEVEN PLANETARY ARCHETYPES

☉ ☽ ♂ ☿ ♃ ♀ ♄

NINE WAYS TO UNDERSTAND
THE SEVEN PLANETARY ARCHETYPES

WE ARE CREATED AS PLANETARY MAN AND WOMAN, IN THE IMAGE OF the seven planets and their associated Planetary Gods/Goddesses and Archetypes: As Above, so below. Our Major Planetary Archetype (our mental, emotional and physical makeup) is based on the day of the week in which we are born and our Minor Planetary Archetype (our physical makeup) is based on the time we are born. (See Planetary Archetype Chart)

Relearning this ancient Planetary Archetype system will help us live healthier lives by interpreting how our mental, emotional, and physical traits are instilled, activated, and managed by our Ruling Planet. This is a system that has held true over millennia, only to be lost to time and history, hidden within science, religion, language, astronomy, astrology, and alchemy and forgotten from the minds and consciousness of the modern human race, before it could be found again and rediscovered. It is time to recognize ourselves and others, and to see ourselves in others, and vice versa.

It is time to remember why we are the way we are. Why do certain behaviors and events repeat themselves again and again, and how can we evolve in order to have greater control over our choices and our destinies?

I propose nine key facets of understanding each of the Seven Planetary Archetypes, and I hope that perhaps readers will find in their own experiences, elements to add to this ongoing and evolving discussion and equation.

- **The Seven Days of Creation and of the Week.** The Bible Story of the Seven Days of Creation is symbolic of the seven days of the week. For example, on the first Day of Creation, which is Sunday, God created light—this symbolic light emanates from the Sun. Each day of the week has its own parallels with its associated Planetary Archetype. For example, when we talk about having "a case of the Mondays," we mean that we feel sleepy, dreamy, and not quite up to the tasks that lie ahead of us in the workweek. The moon, which rules sleep and dreams, is the root of our Moonday/Monday.

- **The Seven Naked Eye Planets.** The Ancients assigned attributes to their Gods and imagined their appearance based on The Seven Naked Eye Planets. For example, Mars, the God of War, is linked to the red, volcanic planet, Mars. This planet is red because it contains large amounts of iron, which is the symbolic metal and tinge of Mars (think war weaponry and blood).

- **The Gods of Myth.** By understanding Gods, Goddesses, demigods, and all of their dramas, challenges, pitfalls, and triumphs, we can learn how we mirror ancient myths and learn moral lessons which can help us more deeply understand their/our corresponding Planetary Archetypes. For example, Mercury is not only a metal and a fast wandering planet, but is also the God that rules communication, language, travel, wisdom, reason, technology and information, as well as deceit, tricks, and cunning.

- **The Archangels or Guardian Angels.** Just as each day of the week has a ruling planet, so too does each day of the week have a guardian angel, or Archangel. We are ruled by one angel, depending on which day of the week we are born on; but, we can call upon any of the angels, any hour or day of the week, for guidance in any particular situation. For example the corresponding Angel for Thursday, or Jupiter, is Sachiel the Angel known for wealth, money, and prayer.

- **The Seven Classical Metals.** The Ancients believed that the seven classical metals were the solidified lights of their corresponding planets. Gold was Sunlight, silver was Moonlight, iron was Mars light, and so on. For example, copper is found in musical instruments, which the Venus Archetype loves and plays.

- **Energy Vortexes and Chakras.** According to ancient teachings, we are created as Planetary Man, complete as tiny universes, or microcosms of the Macrocosm. Each planet rules over and activates one of our energy centers, vortexes, or chakras, which in turn activates and stimulates our organs and organ systems. The seven planets align with the seven chakras in order of the seven days of the week and their corresponding planets. The Sun is the crown chakra, the Moon is the third eye chakra, and so on, ending with Saturn, the root or base chakra.

- **Planetary Age and Hours Cycles.** We age in sync with the seven planets in Chaldean order, or in the order of the planets closest to furthest from the Earth. For example, our first seven years are our Moon years, in which we are all under the influence of the Moon and everything it represents. These seven years cycles continue from birth to death. Each of our days also cycles in the same Chaldean order. The first Planetary Hour, or the Moon Hour, is from 12:00 am to around 3:26 am. During this time, we dwell under the veil of moonlight in the unconscious realm of the brain, sleep, dreams, and psyche. As each day unfolds, so too do the seven planets, each ruling one seventh of the day. Our minor planetary archetype is based on the planetary hour within the day of the week in which we are born. (See Planetary Archetype Chart)

- **The Seven Lost Symbols**

- **The Twelve Astrological Signs of the Zodiac.** Each zodiac sign is ruled by one of the seven planets and Planetary Gods. The Sun rules Leo, the Moon rules Cancer, Mars rules Aries and Scorpio, Mercury rules Gemini and Virgo, Jupiter rules Pisces and Sagittarius, Venus rules Libra and Taurus, and Saturn rules Aquarius and Capricorn. We can use the zodiac to complement what we know from our study of the Seven Archetypes, in order to better understand and be ourselves.

Imagine going through life as One of these Seven Ancient Planetary Archetypes, as that Day of Creation, that Planet, that God/Goddess of myth, that Angel, that metal, that vortex/chakra, that age/cycle, that symbol, that corresponding sun sign or that day of the week, created in the image of that Planet, complete with their "Gift" and "Power" and their mental, emotional and physical traits, qualities and attributes! But we must also travel through life with their "Impotence" and "Folly" (See The Seven Ancient Planetary Archetypes Summary).

Which One are you? Are you ready to learn?

Are you read to look at your Symbol and your SOUL, Spirit and body, in the mirror of the universe?

CHAPTER EIGHT

THE SUN ARCHETYPE

And God said, "Let there be light," and there was light. God saw that the light was good, and he separated the light from the darkness. God called the light "day," and the darkness he called "night." And there was evening, and there was morning—the first day.

—GENESIS

SUNDAY, 10:18 A.M. – 1:44 P.M.

H ALEAKALA, OR EAST MAUI VOLCANO, TOWERS 10,023 FEET ABOVE SEA level. Measured from the ocean floor, it is one of the highest points on Earth. In my mind, this place is one of Maui's seven wonders. In Hawaiian lore, it is said that Maui's grandmother lived in Haleakala's crater and helped him harness the sun to slow its path overhead. The crater is an ideal place to "meditate with the Sun" and to reveal the meaning of Sunday (or "Sun-Day"), the first day of creation, the first day of the week, and the day of the Sun Planetary Archetype.

I sit on the slopes of Haleakala, on a Sunday, during high noon, when the Sun shines brightest and provides the most heat. I am sitting above the tree line, and in my state of calm, I notice the rainbow eucalyptus trees below me do indeed reflect the sun and emit a prism of red, orange, yellow, green, blue, indigo, and violet hues. These trees are aptly named. They are bright and colorful, and their bark glows green. Their colors remind me of an expression of both a smile of happiness and a broken heart of sadness. Just like the monkeypod trees in my home in Haiku and my old friend the banyan tree in Lahaina, the smell of the eucalyptus takes me back to my childhood, captivating the wonders of the world.

I am in Hawaii, but my mind is traveling far from the volcano. What comes to mind is another iconic "mountain-shaped" image: In all of my studies on Egypt, I've read many stories and articles which state that the Great Pyramids were built in the image of the constellation of Orion, a literal mirror image of the Macrocosm in the microcosm; As Above, so below. Whether this is true or not, I do notice that many locations and creations on earth that are symbolic of the heavens, and these places and objects provide us with a greater understanding of the Seven Planetary Archetypes.

If gazing past the bright Sun to see the Moon and the stars were possible, what would become very clear, as clear as the day, is that we can look to the Macrocosm and see seven wandering planets. We know that the Ancients believed these seven stars were the Seven Planetary Gods, our Watchers or Governors, the rulers of Destiny and Fate. We know that Christians adapted their Seven Angels from those same seven planets and those same Seven Planetary Gods of the Ancients. We know that scientists too, discovering that we human beings are made of stardust, have offered us another form of proof that all is connected. From where I stand or sit, from wherever I climb or ride or sail upon the Earth's crust or waters—I am made of the same cells, elements, molecules, atoms and metals as the universe and the seven planets are made of.

Spending a portion of my formative "keiki" years growing up on Maui, I remember many trips rising towards the heights of the Sun on the slopes of Haleakala. Even as we climbed the long and winding road to the top of my world, closer and closer to the sun, no matter what the time of day, or what season, the temperature would drop. The elevation, with its brisk thin air, woke me and gave me the ability to look out over the world, which as a child, I dreamt of as not only my home, but also as my kingdom.

My fascination with Haleakala grew throughout the years when I visited and stayed overnight there with family and various friends. Even in eternally tropical Hawaii, at that elevation, mornings were chilly. I remember being wrapped in blankets, huddling with people and waiting for the sun to rise. The thick black remnants of night would slowly give way, pierced by the sole gleaming eyeball of the universe. Together, we small specks of stardust humans would take a collective in-breath, as light came to start our day, just as Sunday starts our week.

We are warned never to look directly at the sun, and I of course, resisted. But from the corner of my eye, I remember watching the golden orb appear ascend over the horizon and thinking, "This is how God creates "Light." This is the Earth's greatest crown jewel."

What a feeling: the richness of the day was before us. We felt inspired and able to reach whatever dreams we aspired to! Our kingdom and future was lit up as far as the eye and light could see and take us. This is the power the Sun has always held—every day is a new beginning. To this day, my mind and heart connect the Haleakala sunrise and the Maui pineapple. Pineapple is Maui's own gold. Shirts and coffee mugs in Hawaii's retail shops bear a pineapple graphic and the words "Stand tall and wear a crown." The word Haleakala means "House of the Rising Sun."

The Sun Archetype is the Father and is represented by the Shield of Helios and the symbol of gold, among other things. Mental and emotional attributes of the Sun Archetype include warmth, light, happiness, radiance, vitality, leadership, willpower, self-confidence, enthusiasm, honesty, humility, goodness, generosity, and focus. Physically and physiologically, the Sun rules the heart, the circulatory and pituitary systems, as well our eyes and eyesight.

The Sun gives us his Gift of the "Gold Heart, Crown of Light, and Compassion of the Father" with the heart and circulatory activated and the Power of "Warmth." When their Gold Heart is illuminated and they are paying attention to matters of the heart and circulatory system, Sun Archetypes exude love, compassion, energy, power, leadership, and expression. When the heart is dull or discontent and the heart and circulatory system are weak, the Sun Archetype "turns cold" and shuts down.

The Sun teaches us what the Father traditionally teaches us. While the Moon represents the Mother and matters of the home, the Sun pushes us out of the womb and into the world, onto the stage so that we might shine our light. Obviously, we need the Sun and the Moon, the Father and the Mother, the Masculine and the Feminine, the Light and the Dark. Fortunately, these polarities tend to seek balance and we can learn how to balance ourselves better by observing them. Sunday's child is born bonny and blithe, as the rhyme tells us. But they do have to work on taming their desire to outshine everyone all the time. When asking "Who am I? the Sun Archetype needs to listen to the answer, but not sit too long allowing their pride to build!

Apollo, Helios, Sol/Soul, Re or Ra—Dominos, as in Domingo, or Sunday— the God of the Sun, as well as the son of God, pulled the great ball of fire that sustains all life across the sky in a golden chariot. It's a big job, so no wonder the Sun Archetype's ego can get out of hand if not monitored. Being the son of Zeus was no small matter either. Apollo was visited by people from far and wide, who believed he could foretell their futures, heal their wounds and illnesses, and help them stay forever young.

The Sun Archetype is focused on their gold mine, their golden goose and egg, their treasure, their business, or business opportunity, through sales and marketing, investing and investments, assets or through all things that allow them to imprint, or shine their light, or be in the spotlight of the world. They can be materialistic and have their eye on physical gratification which can buy happiness, from houses, or castles, to boats and cars, clothes, watches, jewels and all things that represent riches and richness, success and admiration, which in the long run is about reaching their goals and their gold.

Gold, gold, gold—that is the Sun Archetype's motivation and mantra, and while gold is associated with success, power, and wealth, on its own it cannot bring happiness and fulfillment. For a Sun Archetype to attain sustainable contentment, they must nurture their souls—their sols—as well as their wallets.

The Sun Archetype at its best is the sun that we all drew as children—it wears a smiley face and we all turn our faces toward it. We wish to soak in all of the sun's goodness; we wish to harness it like Maui did and put more hours in our day.

The Sunday child excels at self-expression, outward expression, and spreading joy and wealth. In adulthood, this archetype can be found wherever riches, sound investment strategies, and well-run businesses are incubating. If you have a friend or a colleague that everyone refers to as "The Golden Child," you can bet your money they were born on a Sunday. That person who lights up every room they enter—they're a Sun Archetype. The friend or family member who drenches themselves in gold jewelry, wears their focals, or bi-focals, and wears their sunglasses at night—they are a Sun Archetype, or they wish they were.

I don't have to travel to Hawaii to appreciate the Sun: simply thinking about it warms my skin and heart. I close my eyes, and remember the last solar eclipse I witnessed—how the grass absorbed a pattern of dozens of small shimmering crescent moons; how the temperature dropped steadily; how the birds stopped chattering, singing, and flying. I open my eyes and squint at the Sun, aware that my very own irises contain sun-like rays and elements.

The eyes are the windows to the soul, and the Sol, the Sun, fuels our soul's energy. When we die, our soul departs its bodily cage and we quickly stiffen and turn cold. Warmth is life.

Too much warmth though, is dangerous and deadly. Wildfires ravage our Mother Earth, and though she rebuilds and regenerates on her own accord, things are literally heating up too fast now and entire species—including our own—are at risk. Solar flares, caused by criss-crossing fields of magnetic energy on the Sun, are rumored to be getting larger. The largest solar flares interfere with our technology and cause power outages. We gripe a lot about Mercury Retrograde causing breakdowns in communication, but the truth is, our Sun has the potential to cause way more headaches (and eye aches, skin disorders, and so on), than any other celestial body.

The Sun Archetype is the center of the universe and the center of attention. Sun Archetypes make good leaders and salespeople, and they must be focused to be healthy. A statement I hear often from the mouths of those born on Sunday is "I need to feel appreciated." Tickle Sunday's child ego. Remember they are the "ME ME ME!" people of the universe, and they desire more than any other archetype to be honored, (though they do strive to be level-headed, it is a struggle) although they can be quite humble.

Sunday's children consider themselves Kings (or Queens) of the Kingdom below. And though they are sometimes cocky, they have a heart of gold. When clouds come, they feel depressed, and so sun people who live in Seattle surprise me.

Sun Archetypes are often athletic, some professional athletes, setting records, especially in financial contracts and even earning gold medals. They wear their gold medals and their gold chains around their neck and heart. Gambling, the pursuit of "gold" or winnings can be an issue.

Apollo was not only the Sun God, but the God of light and day. He is known for and honored for driving his golden chariot and horses across the daytime sky until Artemis, the Moon Goddess, showed up and took over with her chariot, pulling the Moon across darkness and the night sky. The Sun and the Moon never fought, for they each had a necessary role in maintaining the health of the planet and all creatures on it. The Sun and the Moon struck a harmonious balance, one I know I strive for in my various adventures, at work, and at home with friends and family.

The Sun God balanced things out not only with the Moon Goddess, but also within himself. His job was to follow the correct trajectory, based on the season of the year and the time of day. Imagine taking the same route to work day in and day out, never veering off course for to try out the new coffee shop or to stop afterwards at a friend's new Happy Hour hot spot. Apollo was committed and focused.

Apollo's chariot was made of such bright, refined gold that no mere mortal could look directly at it. He steered that chariot not too far, nor too close to the Earth. In doing so, he doled out as consistently and as predictably as possible the correct amount of light and heat. We were to be kept warm—warm enough to grow ourselves and to grow things, like pineapples and carrots. But we could not be kept too warm, so that the earth beneath our feet was scorched, crops failed, and sources of water dried up. Again, this God Apollo had a lot on his plate when it came to fueling life.

In one story, Apollo and his son Phaethon must work through a typical father/son struggle—albeit of a Godly weight.

One pre-dawn day, Phaethon demanded that his father allow him to drive his chariot across the sky. Apollo, letting down his usual guard, handed over the reins and then stood back on the sidelines to observe. Did he need a day off, who knows, but boy, did he make a big mistake!

As Phaethon was making his way across the sky, perhaps feeling cocky as the son of the God of the Sun, he forgot about the need to stay the course, to focus. The horses, confused, might have bucked or hesitated. Whatever happened in this great story—and as usual, there are multiple variations of it—as soon as Phaethon lost control of his father's horses, his father's chariot began to veer out of control. Spinning downward in a blaze toward Earth, there was nothing Phaethon could do—he was young and inexperienced. Upon impact, mountains, forests, and even the seas were lit up. Animals and humans alike were scorched. Vast swaths of the planet that day were rendered lifeless and smoke and ash took days to clear.

Zeus, upon seeing this disaster, and in order to save the world, struck his own grandson dead, the son of the Sun God.

Wow, if that's not a reminder to listen to our father's advice as we go out into the world in order to shine our light, I don't know what is.

In all of my studies of ancient myths, the central morals and lessons associated with Apollo (or Helios, Dominos, or Sol) point to loyalty, leadership, and the self. The downfall of the Sun Archetype gone off course can manifest as a case of overblown pride, ego, self-centeredness, and even solitude, loneliness and depression.

Sun children have a gold heart. They emit a crown of light and are fatherly, creative, passionate, enthusiastic, energetic, royal, noble, and inspirational. On the downside, they can be arrogant, overly confident, self-centered, selfish, and coming from a place of "I" or ego. They sometimes may radiate despair and hopelessness.

A well-balanced Sun Archetype, like our never-wavering from his path Apollo, provides just the right amount warmth, heat, and energy, which in turn fosters devotion, love, charm, chivalry, happiness, and smiles.

So now, Sunday's child, you know that you are "bonny and blithe" and "good and gay." But let's push the "Who am I?" question further than that by investigating the nine ways to interpret the Sun Archetype.

1. The Seven Days of Creation and of the Week

If we look at the seven-day creation story, we can see how the words of Genesis contain a symbolic representation of all of the days of the week, including the first day of creation and of the week. On Sunday, God created light. Before that, "the earth was formless and empty, darkness was over the surface of the deep, and the Spirit of God was hovering over the waters."

Once light came, "God saw that the light was good, and he separated the light from the darkness. God called the light "day," and the darkness he called "night." And there was evening, and there was morning—the first day."

Whatever religion we are, or if we subscribe to no religion at all, some element of our soul connects to the notion of light marking the start of something—light is the notification of new possibility.

Sunday is not only the first day of the week and the first day of creation, but also the first Planetary Archetype—the Sun Archetype. When God, our Creator, created Sunday, the Sun Archetype was also born in the image of Sunday and the Sun.

Just as the Sun shines bright in the day, so too, does Sunday. This is the day named after the Sun, and it shines first. It should come as no surprise that Sunday is the first day of creation and the first day of the week. The Sun has to be center of attention—it is the big "show off," always trying to grab our eye.

Sunday is, in many places, a day of relaxation, laziness, rejuvenation, and finding calm. Whether we chill out and play at the beach, or meditate and pray on Sundays, our cells and our souls are cleansing themselves, gathering new energy, and aligning to dance. And of course Sunday is a day to worship the son of God, also known as the Sun of God, or the Sun God. Jesus, or "of Zeus," is the not only the son of God, but also the Sun God.

When I take a Sunday to visit Haleakala, the "House of the Rising Sun," I choose to place myself on what feels like the top of the world. Here, I am as close as I can get to the Sun God, to Mount Olympus, to all of the Seven Planetary Gods, to Heaven and God, our Creator. I choose Sunday as my day, wherever I am, to channel warmth and heat so that I might access the Lords of Cycles, the Lords of Destinies, and the Lords of Fates.

Sunday is the day so many humans across Mother Earth set aside to connect with their version of the "Planetary Butterfly Effect" or the Seven Creative Forces, which cause the ether of the universe to vibrate straight into and through us. We are altered on Sundays, and we seek out solace and guidance at the altar of our choosing.

2. The Seven Naked Eye Planets

Although we can all enjoy the warmth of the sun, only some of us carry the warmth of the sun within us. Sunday's children, like all seven planetary archetypes, are like the ruling planet in which the days of the week were named after. I worship the sun and I respect it. A haole on Maui, I experienced my share of sunburns as a child. I also watched the sun blast through a heavy storm and toss up a double rainbow.

The Sun is made of hydrogen and helium, which is where we get the word "Helios." The Sun emits light, daytime, and warmth. We are as familiar with the powers of the Sun as we are with the powers of the Moon. The Sun is the center of our solar system and universe. The Sun is the center of our bodies—the heart. As Above, so below.

The Sun Archetype is ruled by, and it rules, our organ of warmth, light, love, and compassion. When we speak or act from the heart, we do so under Apollo's guardianship. The heart manages the flow of our circulatory system and our plasma in order to create warmth within us and a warmth we can share with others, in the form of affection, compassion, empathy, or love.

The Sun Archetype is at the center of attention, demanding respect and authority, and to shine brightest. The Sun affects and creates sensitivity in the realm of the eyes and so our vision can be triggered, activated, harmed, or nurtured by the Sun.

The Sun affects our skin, causing burns, rashes, blisters, flakes, or disruptions such as acme and eczema, of the skin.

The Sun and those born on Sundays are connected with anything that is shiny, bright, and sparkly. Just as the Sun circulates through the sky, so too does gold circulate in business and wealth. And just like the sun, every Sun Archetype has a potential to burn too quickly, or to burn others. Being aware of their own force allows them to manage it by seeking shade and places where they can "cool down," chill out, or be soothed.

3. The Gods of Myth

Whether we read about Apollo (Greek & Roman), Sol (Norse) or any of the other names he is referred to around the world—Helios, Re or Ra, or Dominos—the Sun God is the God of light, day, shine, warmth, inspirations and aspirations, success, confidence, business, investment and richness. Looking at the many tales associated with him, we see that they are one and the same—the same myth, the same legend, the same folklore, and the same story. By understanding these tales, we can rediscover and understand the Sun Planetary Archetype.

Apollo only let go of his duty one day, when he allowed his son to give carrying the sun across the sky a shot. It was a dark day, no pun intended. Because of his light, good looks, and glow, humans turned to Apollo to renew their beliefs in everlasting youth. When you think about it, one of the reasons many people still plant themselves on a sunny beach all day despite warnings of skin cancer, is that being tan makes most people look healthier!

To the Ancients, Apollo was not only a curer, a decent musician, and a fortune teller, he was also a fierce protector. On two separate occasions, he slayed a python and then a monster, to defend his mother's honor. He also helped Paris kill Achilles after Achilles killed one of his sons.

There is a fiery loyalty in all Sun Archetypes, and they will just as soon spread a warm smile as the will launch an arrow straight through an enemy's heart.

4. The Archangels or Guardian Angels

Michael, commonly the most familiar of the Angels, is supported by a crew of his own angels, wearing a crown of illuminated golden light, and is a protector and helper. He rules Sunday and brings the Sun whenever and wherever you need it to shine. Need to bring light to a dark situation or burn away the negativity? Call on this angel and you will feel his presence quickly. His light penetrates and surrounds you. Just as the Sun rules our skin, Michael's presence is associated with goosebumps. Under the influence of this Sun-kissed angel, your skin tingles and your heart fills with warmth.

Michael is known to be the Angel of feeling and divine will. He tends to the center of our bodily universe—our heart—and he reminds us that we are loved, no matter what. When we look at an image of Michael, we see him ablaze in golden light, hovering on his golden wings and donning his golden armor, golden shield, and golden sword. Those born on Sunday possess traits of this angel, and when they are functioning at their highest state of being, they do have the power to heal and spread joy.

5. The Seven Classical Metals

The Alchemists taught us that each planet had a corresponding metal, or solidified light, and we are each created with a tinge of the planets. The Sun's metal and tinge is gold. Gold is the metal of wealth, business, investment, inheritance, nobility, honor, pride, regality, standards, respect, morality, authority and kings.

Gold has historically been used to measure worth, literally on ancient scales in ancient ports and tradeposts; and figuratively, in terms of setting the gold standard in a business, invention, or sport. Those who win gold medals stand on a podium heads above the silver and bronze medal winners.

Gold represents the self, one's personality, pride, and ego. An expressive, light capturing and reflecting metal, gold attracts attention. It casts an aura of wealth, regality, and nobility and it is proof that a civilization and its economy are growing. Gold represents an accumulation of material things and materialism.

Sun Archetypes are drawn to the positive facets of gold, and must be aware that acquiring too much of it will not only weigh them down, but may potentially mar the purity of their heart and the source of love and joy. Gold is good and Godly, but, like money, it cannot buy happiness.

6. The Seven Vortexes, or Chakras and Organ Systems

As the planets wander through the heavens, they spin and hum and vibrate with sound, creating an effect that affects us. The planets are in tune with the seven vortexes, or chakras within our bodies, which also spin and hum and vibrate. As Above, so below, these spinning vortexes above and within us are in tune with and are influenced by the Sidereal Seven.

The chakras run down our spine in the same order as the seven days of creation and the seven days of the week, from the Sun, or crown vortex, all the way down to the root vortex, or Saturn. The constant vibration and interaction of these seven vortexes activates the seven organs and organ systems within the body, and so we keep humming and spinning, living and moving and creating and dying.

Our first vortex or chakra is our Sun Chakra, the crown chakra.

Physically and physiologically, the Sun Chakra rules the heart, circulation, the pituitary system, blood, plasma, eyes, vision, vitality, warmth, heat, circulation, the solar plexus, and the pulsing and vibrancy of our blood.

We stimulate or calm this chakra to balance the facilities of the all that we feel. Whenever we are dealing with matters of the heart and blood, the romantic, the heartbreaking, the thrilling, or anything that causes heartburn, we need to turn our attention to the Sun and to this chakra and visualize until we can feel it, the temperature lowering as it does during a solar eclipse.

7. Planetary Age and Hours Cycles

Many of us are familiar with the human seven-year cycle, as originally put forth by Rudolph Steiner: Each of us experiences seven-year-long stages of being and growing, from our earliest developmental years and learning, through to our young adult relationships and careers, and into old age, as our physical and mental health decline.

What many do not know is these cycles are in tune with the seven planets. Think about it: If you were to reflect back on your life to this day, you would likely note major turning points at ages seven, fourteen, twenty-one . . . and so on. This is no coincidence.

As we age, we age in sync with the seven planets in Chaldean order, the order of the planets closest to furthest from the earth. Our first seven years are our Moon years, in which we are all under the influence of the Moon and everything the Moon represents. From age seven to fourteen, we are in our Mercury years, the years in which we develop our minds, ration, reason, language, and communication. From age fourteen to twenty one, in our Venus years: we hit puberty, develop our first crush and love, and begin to take care of our personal appearance.

These seven years cycles continue. In the Sun years, our middle years, we shine bright, so bright that we go through three age cycles from twenty-one to forty-two (I do not know why, as we cannot go back to a Time Before Time when this was common knowledge). In our Mars years, from age forty-two to forty-nine, we begin to first acknowledge our physical mortality. In our Jupiter or "return" years, from age forty-nine to fifty-six, money comes and goes as we focus on retirement and security. In our Saturn years, from fifty-six to sixty-three, we experience decay and entropy. We become aware of death, or of the eternal rest that will eventually fall upon us.

In my early sun years, while managing a restaurant and bar, I considered starting one of my own. Then, I changed careers completely, going into real estate, the mortgage industry, finance, and sales. I was out there in the real world from age twenty-one to forty-two, trying to shine my light, find my own gold, and manage my own identity and ego. Towards the end of my Sun planetary age, I chose to put all I had learned so far about planetary archetypes on paper, so that this ancient gnosis might go out into the modern world and illuminate questions common to all of us, such as "Who am I?"

Just as human beings go through seven-year age cycles, every day also cycles in the same Chaldean order, with each planet ruling one-seventh of each day. Each day is a perpetual recreation of the seven days of creation, from the Moon to Mercury, followed by Venus, the Sun, Mars, and Jupiter. The day "dies" with Saturn at midnight, only to be born again the next day.

The fourth Planetary Hour is the fourth-seventh of the day, from 10:18 a.m. to 1:44 p.m. It is during this time that the Sun shines its light the brightest, and high noon brings the daytime to the center of our universe.

We are focused on our daily activities and express our goals with hope and aspirations of success.

8. The Seven Lost Symbols

From ancient times, we have the seven symbols used to represent the seven planets. The Sun Symbol, ☉, is the Eye, the Eye of God, the Eye of Ra, the Center, the Day, the circlet with emitting rays, the Golden Shield of Helios, the Chariot's Wheel, the Divine Spirit, the Soul, the King, the Crown and the Aura. It is the symbol of gold, the symbol of Sunday, and the ruler of Sunday's child, or the Sun Archetype.

9. The Twelve Sun Signs of Contemporary Astrology

The knowledge and wisdom of the Seven Planetary Archetypes is veiled within the twelve zodiac sun signs of contemporary astrology. The Sun is the Ruler of the Sun Sign of Leo, and Leos are strong, natural born rulers.

Sun Archetypes are similar, in that they, like Leo the Lions, strut through their kingdom, roaring and taking center stage. King of the jungle, Sun Archetypes bask in the sun and leap into action to protect their pride whenever necessary.

Gold is everywhere the Sun Archetype is. It is the color of the king of all animals, again, the lion. The male lion's mane casts an aura of gold—it is an aurora of gold, around the lion's head. If you see someone with a head of hair so lustrous and thick you want to reach out and touch it, you are likely looking at a Sunday's child.

Sun Archetypes, like Leos, are leaders. They are ambitious, businesses oriented, goal oriented and gold oriented. If you are a Sun Archetype, learn Leo and its traits, and you will see yourself in the mirror of the universe.

In Conclusion

The more we study the Sun and the stories associated with its Gods and Goddesses, the more we can mine our own gold, our own brilliance and worth. Our value in our limited time upon Mother Earth depends greatly on our ability to answer the question, "Who am I?" and I will never stop asking this question of myself, and of people I encounter.

Sunday's children aspire to go through life, or to move across the great stage of life, activated, illuminated, and joyful. The Sun Archetype's mind and soul shine and draws others closer. These are the people we know who excel at inspiration, outward expression, outward emotion, self-expression, creativity, happiness, contentment, royalty, hopefulness, sympathy, generosity, aspirations, achievement, and sentimentality. They focus their sights on the goal, their gold, with a big heart and soul, an aura and shine and a humbleness and calmness. They are proud as a peacock. There's goodness there, nobility, regality, a knight in shining armor with a glow and a sense of honor and pride. The Sun Archetype walks into a room with a bright smile, a shine, and brings confidence to all, to succeed, to be better.

Sure, when the Sun "goes down," we sometimes see the underbelly traits of pride, arrogance, self-centeredness, depression, and despair. But the Sun, like the firebird Phoenix, is a master of regeneration. No matter what Planetary Archetype we inhabit, we have the capacity to encompass our strengths and weaknesses, to grow in starts and fits and leaps and bounds, and to shine most of our days.

CHAPTER NINE

The Moon Archetype

And God said, "Let there be a vault between the waters to separate water from water." So God made the vault and separated the water under the vault from the water above it. And it was so. God called the vault "sky." And there was evening, and there was morning—the second day.

—Genesis

Monday, 12:00 a.m. – 3:26 a.m.

I sit in Lahaina Town on a Monday, after midnight, still and quiet, the birth of a new day. I am planted beneath my favorite Banyan tree and the Moon's soft white light fills my eyes so that I imagine they are glowing. I close my eyes and still can feel them emitting a calming eternal energy that is unbreakable, never-ceasing, like the tides the Moon itself controls. Lahaina, my second seven wonder on Maui, is an ideal place to "meditate with the Moon" and to reveal the meaning of Monday ("Moon-Day"), the second day of creation, the second day of the week, and the day of the Moon Planetary Archetype.

From the deepest and darkest ocean floors to the observatories atop our highest peaks, to ancient mysteries of sacred sites and lost cities, from Easter Island to Stonehenge and Machu Picchu, to the Great Pyramids and the Sphinx, to art and history museums, to haunted mansions, to the Bermuda triangle, to a full moon Monday at a Moon Palace resort in Mexico, to movie theatres as well as the proverbial white padded walls of an insane asylum—all of these symbolic locations on earth represent the Moon, and therefore can help us understand the Moon Archetype.

81

Lahaina, Maui, as noted earlier, is influenced by the Moon. It is a moon-bathed sea-soaked town that sleeps in the bosom of the breasts of Hina, the Hawaiian Goddess who dwells in the Moon. Lahaina subconsciously drinks the intoxicating spirits of Hina's silver milk, and all who wander here are gracefully buoyed by her sustenance.

For decades, I have wandered and wondered on the beaches, the trails, and the streets of Maui. I have peered into and explored caves above water and below. I've ridden waves for what felt like hours and have been happily pummeled by the sea—taken out by it, laid flat on my back. Whenever I am in this position, horizontal—or when I am sitting under my familiar Banyan tree in Lahaina—I look up. The people in front of me interest me, but the Heavens that guide them interest me so much more. Locals and tourists mingle, they come and go, ebb and flow; but all we are doing here below—surfing, hiking, meditating, barbequing, playing tourist, or reading a book on the beach—we are doing because the Gods and Goddesses above make it so.

Out in the sweet Hawaiian early morning gazing past the elliptical leaves of the Banyan tree, a tree that has seen the dinosaurs, our birds and sharks descend from come and go, I look up at the Moon. This grey and white sphere is a body in motion and it is one week past being full, on its journey to becoming new. And just as the Moon is weeks away from being new, or "dark," or asleep in the dream world of unconsciousness, I realize that our ancient knowledge and wisdom has also taken this route. What we once knew in the core of our cells has been veiled in darkness, lost to time and history, hidden within science, religion, astronomy, language and mathematics, and erased from the consciousness of the modern human race. The Moon does not stop in its cycle, but somehow, our wisdom has gotten lost and stuck on "the other side."

As the moonlight reflects and ripples across the ocean, I reflect on my mom and I can feel her voice from within. One of the fondest memories that I have of my mother was in teaching me about health, which became the Five Elements of Health, and the most important lesson was about "space" and thought and thoughts. "It is thoughts which lead to words, actions and deeds, therefore be careful with your thoughts," she would say. "Thoughts and thought patterns become things."

"Be mindful of your thoughts" reverberates in my brain to this day.

As much as we know about the Moon and as much as we love to track its size, shape, and arc—as much as we revere its influence over us—there is so much about its nature and its role in our life that we have forgotten. I gaze upon this Maui Moon that is weeks away from being eclipsed in darkness by the shadow of the Earth only so that it can be revealed again, and I think: There is always birth and rebirth. Our ancient gnosis is about to be revealed from the darkness of time and history.

The Moon Archetype is everything you would expect the mother to be: She is fertility and all that it takes to be fertile, from the menstrual systems and cycles, to our internal rhythms and paces, to our ovaries and eggs, to the womb and stomach to the breasts and milk. Born on a Monday or spending time with a Moonday babe, you become aware of everything that a mother provides, from the warm cocoon of the womb to the safety of a crib to the refuge of a home.

The Moon's Child will look after you. This person's urge is to nurse, to protect, to guide, and to create and initiate life. Do you need emotional support, empathy, a shoulder to cry on, or someone to cry with? Find someone born on Monday. This person is someone you can rely on and call *Mom*. So many doctors and nurses were born on Monday, of course! Who else? Whoever looks and watches over us, our psychologists and psychiatrists, tend to be ruled by the Moon.

Who helps us dwell in and reflect on our psyches—you guessed it. The Moon encompasses all of which looks after us mentally, emotionally, and physically. It is the artist, the musician, the writer, the poet, the romantic, the filmmaker, and the photographer.

The Moon is the custodian of the past, and it enables and encourages us to reminisce and remember. Memories are the Moon's domain, and while so much of our focus these days is to "live in the present" and "be present" and "let go of the past," the Moon knows its history and knows history's value.

Memories are sweet. We honor our dearly departed by keeping memory alive, in the form of legacy.

All Moon children are stewards of the night. Though they may have some of the typical fears of monsters under the bed or bad guys behind the bushes, those ruled by the Moon welcome the dark and find comfort there. Darkness is a friend that embraces them with open arms and lulls them into reverie with silence.

The Moon is of nature and all animals and mammals. The wolves bare their fangs and the fly washes its wings—fierce or feeble, wild or tame, all creatures of the Earth and its trees, rivers, oceans, caves, and seas follow the Moon's orders.

Moon Archetypes dance between the maternal and the mad. If you are a Moon Archetype, you may rock your baby to sleep snuggled between your tummy and your breasts, or you may be "off your rocker." You may wear your moon like pearls created from the ocean floor, or you may have lost your "pearls" or your marbles. At either end of this spectrum, you are loved and loving, adored and adorable.

You may write poetry, plays, or songs about your Watcher, the Moon. You speak truth to madness or craziness, and you sometimes play with madness. Under the Moon is where you "dance like nobody is watching" with spirits in the night. It doesn't bother you that this "alternative energy" is your friend or companion at times. Mayhem is about what *may* come, and you invite all possibilities!

You may be fertile and full of eggs and ovaries, or have a cracked eggshell mind. You may have top-notch finely-tuned gut instincts, or you may have something wrong with your gut and stomach.

You may be strong with Luna, and flow with water and emotions in a way that easily and gracefully encompasses those around you. Those seeking intimacy or a closer connection to their own deep feelings and desires will seek you out because of your emotional breadth. Alternately, you may be a lunatic who overflows with emotions and scares people away.

When healthily balanced, you might be all of these things melded together. When slightly out-of-whack, you will come across as slightly wacky. But as long as you keep track of that Moon, you'll always find your way.

The Moon Archetype dwells under the spells and casts them in the name of the Moon and the Moon Goddess—whatever name we call her, whether Dianna, Artemis, Selene, or Luna. Artemis, the Moon Goddess, was also the Goddess of darkness and of the night. She pulled her silver chariot, moon in tow, across the heavens. She was worshipped and appeased in all matters of fertility and childbirth. She helped gave birth to her twin brother Apollo and never had children of her own. She is the mother of all that is wild, all animals, and the hunt. She is known as the protector.

In one myth, Artemis' close friend, Orion the Hunter, brags to her that he could kill every creature on Earth if he wanted to. Gaia, Mother Earth, sends Artemis to kill Orion, which she does. She sends her hounds after him and they tear him into pieces. What better reminder to listen to our Mother's advice, to protect the Earth, and to preserve the animals and creatures we share our planet with. Artemis may be the Goddess of the Hunt, but as keeper of the Moon, she knows all about balance.

The Moon gives us the Gifts of "the Silver Mirror, the Unconscious Mind, the Intuition of the Mother", the brain and nervous system activated and the Power to "Reflect." When the Silver Mirror is full, or clean, clear, and polished, the brain and nervous system are strong, giving the Moon Archetype the ability to Reflect. When balanced, this archetype excels at carrying knowledge, intuition, emotions, perception, dreams, imagination, and ideas. But when the Silver Mirror is cracked, in pieces or phases, the brain and nervous system are weak and the Moon Archetype has a lack of ability to reflect. It can be ignorant, and even crazy to the point of sometimes being unable to leave the safety of their home and connect, act, or move forward.

The Moon Archetype is the guardian of subconscious and the unconscious, with highly in-tuned and highly activated emotions, sensitivity, intuition, dreams, imagination, perceptions, senses, beliefs, moods and memories. Monday's children are creatures of habit, with instincts and a love for the unknown, the mystery, the mystique, the paranormal and supernatural, as well as antiquity, the past and history. Antique shopping, collecting and memorabilia shopping are the Moon Archetype's specialties!

What is the Moon Archetype's downside? Forgetfulness, ignorance, lunacy, wildness, anxiety, fears, superstitions and addictions.

Monday's Child will heal, thrive, and shine by practicing self-awareness and by harnessing the Moon's Gifts.

And so, in order to really know yourself and begin to answer the question, "Who am I?" you must know more than "Monday's child is fair of face." You must know the Moon Archetype has more than just a pale and translucent face with round and concave features and is young and naïve. You must know how to interpret your archetype. Let us now investigate the nine ways to interpret the Moon Archetype.

1. The Seven Days of Creation and of the Week

Looking at our seven-day creation story and our second day of creation and of the week—our Monday—we see in Genesis an image of "a vault between waters to separate water from water, to create evening and morning, or the second day." If we look at this a symbolic message from our ancestors, and remember how water, the night, and morning are ruled by the moon, we can now understand the second day of creation and Genesis in a unique way. The second day of the week, dating back to Genesis, was always *moon day.*

After a typical "time out" on weekends, we sometimes are loath to rise and shine on Monday. We want to hit that snooze button. We want to delay all there is to do on our To Do List. We have a "case of the Monday's" or are feeling sleepy, dreamy, and tired. It is of course the Moon that rules our sleep and dreams.

Is this Monday morning blues effect, a blue Monday, a coincidence or a synchronicity? Nobody says, "Thank the Gods and Goddesses it's Monday." Perhaps it is because Monday is not only named after the Moon, but *is* the day of the Moon, and on this day that the Moon executes its rulership over the earth most powerfully, particularly over those born on a Monday.

2. The Seven Naked Eye Planets

Although we can all like the moon, only some of us are like the Moon. As the silver-gray mirror in the sky, the Moon reflects light. The Moon within us works the same way. Our brain, our silver-gray mirror, gives us our ability to reflect not light, but thoughts. In our gray matter, we toss ideas around, we create, reminisce, dream, and imagine. Our thoughts come and go, shifting sometimes like the tides.

The Moon and the brain, both grey and round or rounded mirrors, also hide things. The Moon and Mondays specialize in mystery, the unknown, and the mystic.

The Moon rules all waters—the oceans, rivers, ponds, creeks, even puddles, and of course, the currents and tides. It is also the Moon that rules over the tides within us, including our menstrual and emotional cycles, influencing too the layer of water around our brains. And just as the moon has historically determined the rhythm of the harvest, so does the moon, within us, determine our fertility. Indeed, the moon everything that is round and life-giving, including the breasts, stomach, eggs and buttocks. Who else but a Moon Archetype would "Moon" you?

The Moon and those born on Mondays are connected with anything that is black and white, or grey. And just like the moon, every Moon Archetype has a "dark side" they must be aware of, embrace, and manage by seeking light.

3. The Gods of Myth

The moon is known to symbolize a wide range of Gods and Goddesses, including but of course not limited to Artemis (Greek), Dianna (Roman), Mani (Norse) Hina, Luna, Selene and Isis. In almost all cases, she is the Mother Goddess and the Virgin Goddess (it is possible to be both). She is the Queen, the Huntress with Silver Bow and Arrows. In art, she is rarely represented without an animal or two by her side. In Hawaiian myth, Hina is often portrayed with sea turtles and fish, drawing water upwards as she hovers in the space between land and sky.

She is the ruler of the night, dark, sleep, dreams, fertility, childbirth, the harvest, hunt, and wild, all of the animals, mammals, fish, creatures, horned beasts and night critters of the world, as well as the water, the oceans, the seas, tides and floods.

4. The Archangels or Guardian Angels

Gabriel sings lead in the angelic choir and is the ruler of Monday, the day of the Moon. He is known to be the Angel of the psychological. He tends to our dreams and to the feminine, including conception and birth as the initiator of life. He also imbues those who pay attention to him—and to their Guardian celestial body—psychic abilities and intuitive powers. Those who linger under the Moon are adept with casting prophesies and visions, as Gabriel prophesized the end of the world to Daniel, along with the virgin birth of Jesus to Mother Mary.

5. The Seven Classical Metals

The Moon's metal and tinge is silver. Diana/Artemis, Goddess of the Moon, carried a silver crescent-shaped bow and silver arrows. Many people of the Moon Archetype are drawn to silver, whether in jewelry, home décor and accents, or musical instruments. Silver is the metal of dreams and dreamers, and it is used in photography and film to bring visions and imagination to life.

Silver is found in scopes, including telescopes that our esteemed vision-ary Galileo used to peer into the unknown regions of space. The silver and the mirrors in microscopes give us access to the secrets of the biology of life. When nurses put a stethoscope to our chest, they peer into us to understand how we are living. When a filmmaker creates their stories to life, it is dis-played on the silver screen in a dark theatre. When a photographer births their images, it is out of the water of the silver nitrate in a dark room. When we rush out the door on Monday morning, we check ourselves in the mirror, we peer at our reflection, and we see answers to the question, "Who am I?"

6. The Seven Vortexes, or Chakras and Organ Systems

Our second vortex or chakra is our Moon chakra, the Third-Eye, the pineal or the brain Chakra. Physically and physiologically, the Moon chakra rules the brain, the nervous system, the womb and the fertility system. It is in charge of our waters and fluids, our breasts, our stomach and our cycles and rhythms. It influences intuition, perception, senses, beliefs, awareness, receptivity, and impressionability.

We stimulate or calm this vortex to balance the mental facilities of the cerebral complex, including cognition, clarity, insight, visions, lucidity, dreaming, and imagination.

7. Planetary Age and Hours Cycles

I don't remember being born. I was just a baby floating in the universe of my mother's embryonic fluid, awaiting my time to pushed and pulled into the world. I don't remember much of my early moon years either, but I know that I was held, with my youthful, round, and translucent face close to mom's stomach and breasts. I was nourished by my mother's milk.

From there, as my brain, nervous system and dendrites formed, I spent years crying, sleeping, and dreaming. My first memories, as hard as it is to lift the veil of the past and remember, are from about age three, shortly before we moved to Maui. The earliest memories I have are from my mom reading me nursery rhymes and bedtime stories before I drifted off into the embryonic fluid of the universe, to sleep and dream.

Our first seven years are ruled by the Moon, our moon. Everything that the Moon represents, from birth, to our past and ancestry, to our homes, our mothers, to sleeping and dreaming and real-life photos that hold images for eternity. These are our baby years, our emotional beginnings, our crying years and the years our brains develop. We spend these years "mirroring" our surroundings and our family, especially our mothers.

The first Planetary Hour is the first seventh of the day, from 12:00 a.m. to 3:26 a.m. the birth of the day. During this time, the Moon glows above as we are dreaming and sleeping below in the unconscious world of the mind.

8. The Seven Lost Symbols

The Moon's Symbol, ☽, is the Crescent Moon, as well as the Mirror, the Reflector, the Night, the Fertile Crescent, the Fair of Face, the Man in the

Moon, the Phase, and the Horn of the Cow. It is the symbol of silver, the symbol of Monday, and the ruler of Monday's child, or the Moon Archetype.

9. The Twelve Sun Signs of Contemporary Astrology

The knowledge and wisdom of the Seven Planetary Archetypes is veiled within the twelve zodiac sun signs of contemporary astrology. A Moon Archetype is very much like a Cancer—as the moon rules over the sign of Cancer.

Cancer is represented by the crab, a shelled but tender animal. In the deep dark unconsciousness of the sea, it hides within its home, protecting its sensitive emotional, watery side. Its feelings and emotions are not exposed for all to see and prey on. The crab, when approached, can be "crabby."

Moon Archetypes are known for their moods. They are sensitive, emotional, instinctive, and overflowing with feeling. Just as Cancer is the mother and ruler of the home, family and ancestry, so too, is the Moon Archetype. Just as Cancer is a watery, emotional sign full of internal feelings, moods, instincts, intuition, sentiment and sympathy, so too, is the Moon Archetype. Just as cancers love to be fertile like the crab, to grow and provide a home, and to hide in their shells at home, so too, is the Moon Archetype. And just as Cancers love to be fertile, to protect and provide a home for their children, so too, does the Moon, the mother, the protector. If you are a Moon Archetype, learn Cancer and its traits, and you will see yourself in the mirror of the universe.

In Conclusion

The more we learn about the Moon as a celestial body and the more we understand and believe in all its associated Gods and Goddesses, the more we can balance the mental and emotional energies and the more we can power up and efficiently and effectively use our "motherboard."

The Moon Child runs wild with water, with emotions and feelings. We can regulate our emotions and feelings, as well as our moods, dreams, imagination, perception, and awareness to bring about growth and positive change.

We can bear the fruits of our labor or of our loins—that is, we can create and invent, and we can literally conceive, bear, nurture, and raise children.

A Moon Archetype may have clarity of the mind, be perceptive, intuitive, instinctual, or receptive and perceptive. You may have a vivid imagination and recall lucid dreams. You may be in tune with and understand the cycles and rhythms of life and organisms. You may be a romantic lover of poetry, photography, history, and architecture. You may love silver and wear lots of silver. You may be a fan of the "silver screen," our dream world of movies.

You may have studied with scopes and have an interest in biology, medicine, the brain, the psyche, and the neural sciences. You might be the inventor, the creator, the genius and the computer programmer. You may program your brain, or help others do so, as they have the ability to get into someone's mind and psyche. The trick, of course, is to stay out of one's own mind and psyche. You may be intrigued by the mysteries of life, the unknown, and the hidden. You might be a poet, a novelist, a movie maker, a musician or singer/songwriter tapping away at the black and white keys of the piano. You keep a diary.

You may be a doctor, a nurse, a counselor, a psychologist, or a psychiatrist. You might wear the white robe with the symbolic staff of medicine and the silver stethoscope.

Or you might be spacey, unable to sleep, or you sleep too much. You may have anxiety, nightmares, delusions, hallucinations, paranoia, fears, and phobias. You may suffer from memory loss and addiction. You may be crazy.

But all of us, no matter what day we are born on, have a bright side and a shadow side, just like the Moon itself. Self-awareness is quality we should all strive to achieve and to put into practice.

CHAPTER TEN

THE MARS ARCHETYPE

And God said, "Let the water under the sky be gathered to one place, and let dry ground appear." And it was so. God called the dry ground "land," and the gathered waters he called "seas." And God saw that it was good.

Then God said, "Let the land produce vegetation: seed-bearing plants and trees on the land that bear fruit with seed in it, according to their various kinds." And it was so. The land produced vegetation: plants bearing seed according to their kinds and trees bearing fruit with seed in it according to their kinds. And God saw that it was good. And there was evening, and there was morning—the third day.

—GENESIS

TUESDAY, 1:42 P.M. – 5:10 P.M.

HALEAKALA CRATER, ALSO KNOWN AS "RED MOUNTAIN," IS A MIRROR image of Mars on Earth. It is my third seven wonder on Maui and the ideal place to "meditate with Mars," reveal the meaning of Tuesday ("Tius–Day")—the third day of creation, the third day of the week, and the day of the Mars Planetary Archetype.

Giant ancient Mount Haleakala—which forms 75% of the island of Maui— houses multiple ecosystems, each of which is replete with its own unique beauty, flora and fauna, curiosities, risks, and temptations. At the base of the "volcano proper," you wander through either dry forest or rainforest, depending whether you are on the leeward or windward side. Above these forests—threatened by and now protected against invasive species, including humans—you encounter subalpine shrublands, where Hawaii's famous silverswords grow.

In Haleakala's alpine Aeolian zone, all appears barren. Walking the switchbacks to the summit, all you hear is the crunch crunch crunch of your own feet hitting the cinder trail. Your body cools consistently as you walk through clouds of mist to reach the edge of the crater.

On elementary school field trips that took us down into the crater, via Sliding Sands Trail—or Keonehe'ehe'e Trail—my friends and I imagined we were astronauts or space explorers that had landed on Mars. Vast swaths of lava rock, red, orange, or rust, were littered with oddly sculptural broken-spine-like outcroppings of darker sharper rock.

On our "pseudo-Mars," fueled with curiosity and pumped up with pre-pubescent pent up energy and adrenaline, we became rough and tumble competitive kids: We played "King of the Hill" throwing our challengers off our own iron laden little mountains of cinder cone. Who could race to the next point of interest first? Who would scramble up a ridge faster? Who could throw a rock the furthest? We fell, cutting and bruising our knees and palms. Blood flowed and pooled like lava flows and pools.

At that altitude, a cold gray all-encompassing cloud could blow in at any time without warning. My classmates and I would pull another layer out of the backpack our parents had sent us to school with—a sweater, a hat, or a jacket—but being prepared and warm did nothing to counter the effect of feeling weightless, directionless, and suspended in space.

When these trips came to an end, back atop the ridge and preparing for our trek back to our school bus, my teachers, my classmates, and I could simultaneously view the Earth that sustained us, and the Earth that seemed completely foreign to us—wholly planetary, celestial, and magic. We could see for our own eyes how all the planets were connected. We had no clue then that one day far into the future, in 2018 to be exact, NASA's Mars Exploration Rover *Opportunity* would find and photograph rock stripes on the surface of Mars that were similar to rock stripes found on another of Hawaii's famous volcanoes, Mauna Kea.

The air is so still atop Haleakala, there were days then and there are days now when I am up there and I am not Earth-bound. Haleakala last erupted in the 17th century, and walking it, there is more risk of acquiring altitude sickness or being stung by wasps than there is experiencing an active eruption. Astrophysicists work atop the mountain, using some of the most powerful telescopes in the world, in what is known as "Science City." There, where there is very little light pollution, they study the stars and the growth of light pollution, among other things.

The light—the sun's light—when it rises over Haleakala's crater walls is mesmerizing. Thousands of tourists bid for permits to camp overnight and experience the sky's intense shift from total darkness to glorious orange, red, and gold. Thousands more wake early, pack a picnic breakfast, and drive up, all to start their day honoring Maui—the demigod who lassoed the sun to slow its journey over the islands.

But once the sun blazes overhead in all its glory, the red sparseness of this crater and the colors found in Pele's Paint Pot call Mars to mind, for me. The sword Mars carried, I see in the silverswords. The Hawaiian Islands are filled with sacred and evocative spaces, and this is why whenever I return to Maui, I return to the mind space where I ask, once again, "Who am I?"

Mars is the Warrior, and is represented by the male symbol of the Shield and Sword, which is also the symbol of iron—the mineral that gives blood its red color and that oxidizes in rocks when exposed to the elements, turning them red, orange, and rust.

Mentally and emotionally, Mars is the Ruler of strength, energy, athleticism, passion, aggression, anger, drive, bravery, impulsivity, survival, and ambition. Physically and physiologically, Mars is the ruler of the blood and immune system (our defense system), blood pressure, the arteries, tendons, muscles, the gall bladder, adrenals and adrenaline and iron.

Mars is the God of sport and athletics. Football is played on a gridiron. In basketball, the best of the best players slam-dunk "on the iron" and players will say, about a weak shot, that it "barely drew iron." Hockey players protect, defend, and score on a goal made of steel, which is an alloy of iron and carbon. Baseball is played on a diamond of red dirt with bats made from trees that grew in our iron rich soil—trees that were grown from the masculine seed.

Golfers choose their club—their iron—depending on the terrain in front of them, the distance their golf ball must travel, the direction and strength of the wind, and the quality of air that day. They choose their iron too, based on their level of expertise in the sport—how good is their swing, their aim, their judgment? How confident are they, with that "sword," so capable of cutting or slicing, in their hand?

The pugilist, the boxer and the fighter, train to hit and strike with precision. Their combat is an art and a blood sport; it is the "sweet science" of toughness and tactic.

For centuries, blacksmiths have hammered—with their blood, sweat, and muscle—iron and steel on their anvils to mold weaponry. Mars brings out the power of war that dwells in our histories and in our bones, and when we honor our war veterans, we honor and remember Mars too. Mars Archetypes beat their own drums, march to their own drumbeat, and lead us into war with the sound of marching feet and sticks on skins.

The friend that is into action and adrenalin sports and waits for the hurricane-level storms to roll ashore and bring the big surf, and then drops everything to ride waves all morning—"cowabunga"—is a Mars Archetype. The friend who jumps without hesitation off the cliff into the sea, or over a bridge into one of Maui's waterfall pools, is ruled by Mars. The colleague who runs or is at the gym when it opens at 5:00 a.m. to pump iron, to get their blood and adrenalin flowing, and to develop their physicality, muscles and strength, is a Mars Archetype. Drawn to muscle cars, or those who drive fast and furious, live life in the fast lane and need action are influenced by Mars. And the friend that is anemic in life and action, lives life on the other side of the sword, on the passive opposite side, is also ruled by Mars.

Mars Archetypes make good leaders because they dive right in and "attack" problems. They work hard, live hard, and play hard. Passionate masculine energy fuels all Mars children, whether they are male or female, just like it did on our childhood field trips to Haleakala, when we were roughing ourselves up and exploring without fatiguing, despite the thin air.

When I hike the higher altitudes of Haleakala now, as an adult, I slow down. Many people, like me, make the trek through the crater in a day, our blood pulsing through our arteries. We test our endurance, stamina, and fitness, fighting muscle fatigue and inflammation in our Achilles heels, to make it back to the top. As a child, my mom taught me the importance of movement, exercise, being active and working on our fitness. Whether we engage in sports, running, walking and hiking, or the passive sports of yoga, tai chi or qigong, stimulating the blood and muscles and boosting energy and endurance is of much importance to enhance our lives in order to take life by the horns and tackle our everyday challenges.

A hike on Haleakala is never the same, and over the years, sadly, I've noticed the decline in the number of silverswords. It is said that long ago, these plants covered the ground like snow. But now, when I spot a silversword—a plant that is in the daisy family and that can live up to fifty years or more in places few other plants can survive—I take pause. Between destruction caused by invasive species such as cows, goats, and humans, and drought across the islands, silverswords have become a threatened species—they are fighting for survival, as we all are.

There are only three types of silverswords in the world, and they are all found on the Hawaiian Islands. Each species of silversword is unique to a specific volcano. Finding a Haleakala silversword, I sit near it and meditate, but do not disturb it. This is a plant that blooms up to six-foot tall with brilliant purple flowers once in its lifetime, and then dies.

Seeing a silversword in bloom, I reflect on what it means to live and thrive on the edge . . . of a volcano, of an island or continent, of this planet, of our human race. As a child of the Earth, have I fulfilled the role I was meant to fulfill? How and where have I planted myself, grown, blossomed, withered, and come back to life?

The Mars' Child is agile and graceful, athletic, sometimes elegant and divine. They are drawn to swords and guns, or artifacts of war and combat. Out of balance, of course, their testosterone-laden nature can wreak havoc, but when they temper themselves, they fight the good fight. Mars Archetypes, with the sword or scalpel, are deft in battle, leaving the least amount of damage as possible while getting the job done. Mars most definitely lives by the sword and dies by the sword, representing the duality and the nature of Nature.

Who leads a team to victory or speaks the truth when others balk or falter? Mars does. Mars is our friend who knows martial arts, and who will defend us against tough guys in a dark alley, opponents on the playing field, or against our sworn enemies.

Mars is our military and our military is Mars. The army, the armed services, the armory, all of our weapons and arms of war, from ancient to modern times has been under the rulership of Mars. We are led into battle with the voice of Mars and we are led into revolutions by revolutionaries like Mars: "Get up stand up, stand up for your rights!"

Mars enables and encourages us to cheer others on, loudly. Our voice is the most powerful weapon that we can yield—it is our strength and our gift to command and lead. But it is also our folly of anger and hatred, of screaming and yelling, of turning fiery red and of reaching our boiling point. We find our voice via Mars and many great singers, vocalists, rappers, and speakers are Mars babies.

Mars gives us the gifts of the "Iron Blood, the Muscle and Voice of the Warrior", with the blood and immune system activated and the Power of "Strength."

When iron pumps as it should, the blood and immune system are strong, giving the Mars Archetype strength. When balanced, this archetype is graceful and masculine, excelling at sport and war and presenting a strong defense system, survival instincts, assertiveness, confidence, and the ability to compete and lead.

On the downside, when the blood boils, Mars carries aggression, anger, temper tantrums, destruction, and terror.

The gall bladder and the adrenals are ruled by Mars, and when we speak of "having the gall" to do something, we activate the Mars Archetype. Our fight or flight response, activated by adrenalin, saves us from attack or puts us smack dab in the middle of a brawl, whether it be verbal or physical.

When Mars is out of tune, our voice cracks. We experience inflammation, hot flashes or hot spots, throbbing, redness, burns, swelling, shock, or trauma, our immune system gives in. Because Mars is so closely linked to athleticism and sporty endeavors, so too are sprains, injuries, and bruises.

It is in all Mars Archetypes to excel at sports, but taming the fire that rises during challenges or competitions is key. At their best, Mars Archetypes are protectors and defenders. At their worst, they are simple thugs.

Our libido—our fire—is Mars' domain. It is our masculinity. We explode with anger and with joy and passion thanks to the influence of this planet. It is no coincidence that the "sword" of the symbol for Mars mirrors male genitalia.

The Mars Archetype dwells under the spell of Mars, or Ares, Aries, Tiu, or Vulcan, (from which we get the word "volcano"). Whichever title you prefer, when speaking of Mars, you are speaking of the God of war, battles, and volcanoes. Some believe that the planet Mars was once in a continual state of boiling red eruption.

Mars is the God of strength, vigor, and endurance. If you are participating in an Ironman triathlon, you will need to channel this God's power, or run, swim, and bike with a crowd of Mars Archetypes. If injured, it is the one whom wears the "red cross", the symbol of emergency and first aid that comes to our rescue.

While Mars is at times destructive, ultimately, he seeks to bring about peace and stability, usually at the cost of war or by the hand of the sword. He will cull the herd so that the herd remains strong and thriving. Blood red is the color of the robes Mars sometimes wears, and blood will flow and pump through the veins of the living as they eat, breathe, dance, make love, fight, and die.

Who are you if you are a Mars Archetype? You are more than the Tuesday's child that "is full of grace." Let us now investigate the nine ways to interpret the Mars Archetype.

1. The Seven Days of Creation and of the Week

Looking at our seven-day creation story, and at our third day of creation—our Tuesday—Genesis presents us with an image of terra firma, or "firm land" and "solid ground." We see in Genesis, "dry land appear." Here, I have an image of plate tectonics and volcanos, powerful and fiery, moving land to form continents. I associate Tuesday and Mars-day with mass, soil, dirt and rocks. From there, the masculine "seed" is formed and nurtured properly, it grows into plants and trees. Continuing the Martian-like full circle, many of these trees are then cut by the sharp iron and steel axes that graze the end of wooden handles, to make more wooden handles for yet more axes—which of course were some of our earliest weapons and which now are instruments of utility and sport. From Terra Firma to the male seeds of creation, Tuesday, the third day of creation, was seeded and created in the image of Mars.

After Sunday's chill time and Monday's blues, comes Tuesday. After the lag and drag of Monday, most of us feel ready to tackle whatever the world throws at us on Tuesday. We begin in earnest to tick tasks off our To Do lists. We make the calls we need to make and have the challenging conversations we need to have. Though Monday is the traditional start of the workweek, most of us know that we really only put the pedal to the metal when Mars enters the room, or when iron enters our bloodstream. It should come as no surprise that in the United States, we elect our commander in chief, our leader, our "Superman," on Super Tuesday.

2. The Seven Naked Eye Planets

Although we can all fight like Mars, only some of us fight as Mars. Mars, due to its high iron content, is the red planet. Olympus Mons, the largest volcano in the universe, calls Mars home. Mauna Kea doesn't come close in size or power in terms of its potential for explosiveness and fiery destruction.

It is the planet that gives us the word "Martian," the generic term for all space beings we imagine are out there flying around in silver UFOs or Robin Williams' Mork-style eggs, especially those we fear will attack or invade. In 2018, a dust storm that encircled the entire planet of Mars obliterated all connection with NASA's fifteen-year old Opportunity Rover. *Opportunity* had survived a bigger storm earlier in its career, but with Mars being Mars, eventually the planet won. Mars Archetypes often create storms, or storm off in anger. But they also fascinate us and draw attention to themselves—by wearing red, putting on a dramatic show, and running hot, for example—as does our neighborly planet.

3. The Gods of Myth

Mars, also known as Ares (Greek), Mars (Roman), Tyr (Norse), Tiu and Vulcan, is the God of war, sports, courage, competition, victory, strength, passion and the masculine. Ares was not always a particularly popular God, mainly because of his penchant for conflict. He seemed only to show his face in times of war, and his raging temper and tendency to jump directly into action without thinking didn't earn him many friends.

But of course, Ares and his skills and temperament were needed. So what if in the Trojan War he didn't seem to care what side he was on? So what if he liked blood and it didn't matter to him whose blood was drawn? In most battles, he didn't care who won—some Gods, and some people, are like this.

Because Ares did not always fully join with or commit to one side during battle, he was sometimes seen as cowardly, finicky, or untrustworthy. In his best days, Ares could win and lose with respect; but on his worst days, he was somewhat of a crybaby, calling "foul" and "no fair."

In art, Mars is represented as a virile and handsome young man. Even when he is nude or semi-nude, he carries his sword and shield—showing that he is tough enough to go to battle without a coat of full armor!

4. The Archangels or Guardian Angels

Camael is the angel of war, strength, and courage. Often pictured in, or with, a ball of fire with a flaming sword in hand, he is in charge of over ten thousand fiery angels of destruction and is considered to be the leader of the army that expelled Adam and Eve from the Garden of Eden. Being as fiery as Mars, he is responsible for the delivery of the divine spark of love. He imbues those who call upon him renewed passion and ferocity.

5. The Seven Classical Metals

Mars' tinge is iron, the mineral and the metal of blood, war weapons, sports and the machinery used by warriors and athletes. Iron is used to make guns, bombs, submarines, and tanks. It is also a necessary component of blood. When iron-rich blood flows normally and the immune system is strong, Mars shows up with strength, fire, passion, and energy. When blood boils and "heats up" iron, or when the immune system is weakened, the Mars Archetype becomes feeble and anemic.

6. The Seven Vortexes, or Chakras and Organ Systems

Our third vortex or chakra is our Mars, fire, or throat chakra. The Mars Archetype is our voice, our jugular, and our throat. We are vulnerable here, but also mighty. When threatened, we yell and scream. When practicing martial arts, we use our throat muscles to forcefully grunt.

Our throat chakra gives us song, wailing, cheering, screaming, and moaning. We can "go for the throat" or bring someone to ecstasy with a kiss on the neck. When we are angry or excited, arteries bulge at this chakra.

Physically and physiologically, the Mars chakra rules our blood and immune system, our muscles and tendons, our gall bladder and adrenals and our ability of defense as a biological system. Anger, will, volatility, determination and survival instincts rage in this chakra.

In terms of the anger that is associated with Mars, acknowledging it, understanding where it comes from, and processing it allows for a healthy and natural balance.

7. Planetary Age and Hours Cycles

I am currently in Mars Age, or in my Planetary Age between forty-two and forty-nine. These are the "afternoon years" of our lives, the years in which we come out of our sun-centered middle years. In this time period, I have figured out my business and my inheritance in life, which is to share this ancient gnosis of the Seven Planetary Archetypes with the modern world. In this Mars Age, I have accompanied my determination with action. Nothing can stop me in my "Mars mission" to fulfill what Paolo Coelho calls our "Personal Legend" and Napoleon Hill calls our "Definite Purpose in Life."

At the same time I am motivated and fueled with clarity, for the first time ever, I am dealing with my physical mortality and am facing the challenges associated with losing strength, muscle tone, and energy. My body gives more easily in to injuries and accidents and takes longer to recoup from exercise. Cuts and bruises take longer to heal. In general, years of action and adventure, from surfing and skiing to hiking and biking, to accidents and car accidents and head injuries, are all beginning to catch up with me. I have lost a step; I've lost some of my gracefulness. But in order to keep going—to keep marching to Mars' drumbeat—I've learned to call on Mars and to engage with him and everything he represents. I have a new relationship with this aspect of my being, and now work to maintain my health, fitness, and strength through the peaceful sports of yoga, tai chi, chi kung, and stretching.

After high noon and lunch comes afternoon, and the Mars Planetary Hour, from 1:44 p.m. to 5:10 p.m. This is our time to "just do it" and get things done. This is the productive afternoon of our daily lives, where we can compete, complete, and win the day before heading home for dinner. Of course, for many of us, this includes battling rush hour on our journey home, through traffic and road rage, the aggravation time of day.

8. The Seven Lost Symbols

Mars' symbol, ♂, is the symbol of iron, the symbol of Tuesday, and the ruler of Tuesday's child and the Mars Archetype. It is the symbol for the male, and it consists of a shield and a sword, or spear, which stands tall and erect, at attention, in salute, in battle and in war, and of course in sex and love as the masculine.

9. The Twelve Sun Signs of Contemporary Astrology

One of Mars' guides is the woodpecker, a bird known for using its strong beak to get at what it needs (sustenance). The Mars Archetype carries armor and relies on strong allies, like the woodpecker, to manifest what it wants. Mars Archetypes are known for taking the initiative and being able to achieve whatever goals they set for themselves.

The Sun Signs associated with Tuesday's Child, or with the Mars Archetype, are Aries and Scorpio. Like Aries, Mars Archetypes can be impulsive risk takers. Just as Aries is the undeterred "blindly optimistic" powerhouse of the zodiac wheel, so too, is the Mars Archetype.

Just as Aries loves to scale all ladders to the top, so too, does the Mars Archetype. And just as Aries will battle for the number one position with a direct and straightforward approach which at times borderlines on pure greed or selfishness, so too do Tuesday's children. Yes, they might also barrel right over everyone—with grace.

Like Scorpio and the scorpion, Mars Archetypes like to plan and execute attacks via strategic stings and lethal venom. Scorpios are known for being passionate and powerful, so too are Mars Archetypes. In fact, the intensity and masculine sexuality of those born under these influences can overwhelm others, and must sometimes be tempered.

If you are a Mars Archetype, studying up on Aries' and Scorpio traits will help lead you to answers to the question "Who am I?"

In Conclusion

The more the Mars Archetype learns about Mars as a celestial body and the more we understand and believe in all its associated Gods and Goddesses, the more we can curtail the urge to either take flight or to fight. Anger, aggression and aggravation are essential aspects and elements of human nature and human society. As much as some loathe war, it has forever been a part of human history. The flip side of war is, of course, peace. And the positive side of aggression is assertiveness and the drive to take action and accomplish what needs to be done. They are healthiest when they are in shape, fit, and ready to fight the fight. They are their weakest when they are anemic in life, lacking muscle, blood and vigor.

A Mars Archetype may be the most cheerful face at the party and they may always seek the most direct route to their goal and destination. They may be less astute when it comes to navigating nuances, but deep down, they seek order and peace. They make excellent athletes, police, and fire fighters (of course!), but also are found in the military, management, and marketing. Because they take risks and live by the seat of their enthusiastic pants, they make excellent entrepreneurs. Because they take the direct approach—they see a problem, they remove it—they make excellent surgeons. Skilled with the steel blade, they are great chefs—some are iron chefs.

They are heroes and heroines, all capable of super strength and feats: Ironman, Superman, Wonder Woman, and Captain Marvel.

People ruled by Mars, like all of us, have unique ways of bringing their own balance and harmony to the world. From the "ABC's" of Mars we have the alpha, the ambitious and the assertive; the bold, the brave, and the brash; and the competing, the courageous, and the conquering. When Mars Archetypes understand themselves more completely, they truly can lead the charge toward victory and winning.

CHAPTER ELEVEN

THE MERCURY ARCHETYPE

And God said, "Let there be lights in the vault of the sky to separate the day from the night, and let them serve as signs to mark sacred times, and days and years, and let them be lights in the vault of the sky to give light on the earth." And it was so.

God made two great lights—the greater light to govern the day and the lesser light to govern the night. He also made the stars. God set them in the vault of the sky to give light on the earth, to govern the day and the night, and to separate light from darkness. And God saw that it was good. And there was evening, and there was morning—the fourth day.

—GENESIS

WEDNESDAY, 3:26 A.M. – 6:52 A.M.

THE WIND BLOWS STRONG IN PAIA, MAUI, AND PEOPLE BLOW THROUGH this town and across the island every year as they traverse the globe, seeking beauty, peace, wilderness, adventure, and the offbeat. In the minutes between darkness and light, night and day, the wind blows the early morning clouds away as the last stars and planets skim the sky and space revealing the new day that is before us. Paia Town is my fourth seventh wonder on Maui and the ideal place to "meditate with Mercury," reveal the meaning of Wednesday (or "Wodens-Day"), which is the fourth day of creation, the fourth day of the week, and the day of the Mercury Planetary Archetype.

I venture out early and hear a few planes landing and taking off from the airport. Soon, kitesurfers—hovering and floating as if they are weightless, saintly, and otherworldly—will perform acrobatics midair. Up the road, lean wind-sculpted windsurfers will rip across the Pacific Ocean at Ho'okipa

Beach Park. On the North Shore surfers will hang all their cares in the world out to dry as they catch some of the largest waves in the world.

The multihued cozy little town of Paia is under the influence of Mercury, the God of travel, commerce, change, speech, communication, air, and wind. This is a town that breathes in its own secret elixir of elements and bathes everyone in a glowing cloud of openness. Stores and storefronts have changed hands and commerce over the years. Shopkeepers, locals, and visitors here are all equally inspired by, in tune with, and inebriated on life.

In Paia, birds glide on the wind and land on the telephone wires, displaying their dexterity, balance, and tendency to flock together. The birds constantly watch, squawk, chatter, and swap song or stories, like the people in the streets: As Above, so below.

Paia is a town where one is aware of the wind moving through their lungs, ears, mouth, throat, and nose—where one is completely conscious of their mind being freed from ration and reason. The town is a barometer of the human race, where locals, travelers, performers, comics, actors, singers, nerds, geeks, intellectuals, hippies, thieves, swindlers, and tricksters gather. It is a town of many personalities and voices, and if one is not grounded, one can become easily distracted, at the mercy and whim of the wind.

I remember as a young boy, visiting the sole electronics store in Paia. In my entirely hands-on world of sand, sea, and salt, of climbing trees and exploring rock formations and caves, this shop was one of the few places where I experienced technology. My dorky, geeky, intellectual side was curious and thrilled by televisions, VCRs, and computers, and one of my first loves—video games. My family would do what we needed to do with the expert techie behind the counter; we would hook up to what we needed to hook up to in order to stay in contact with the faster-paced world.

Computers awed me, with their programs, hardware, software, RAM, DOS, wires, motors, drives, cords, and the sounds and beeps of their language. Sometimes, feeling machine-like or robotic myself inside, I glommed onto all things technological and logical with a keen sense to learn and understand with the ability to just think things through and figure them out. Using ration and reason, computing angles and percentages, and analyzing and interpreting all around me was how I filled much of my time when I was not out exploring the natural world. Now, I can hold all of my childhood technology and electronics in the palm of my hand, on one device, made from the same natural world of "sand," or silicon, of the beaches I enjoy.

Of course, I learned to balance my tech time with my fresh air and outdoor time. Watching people play and float in the ocean never gets old for me. I still am in awe of surfers, windsurfers, and kitesurfers. Children building castles at water's edge lose themselves in that sound and space too. In places like Paia, if you squint toward the horizon, you can almost hear the ancient Hawaiians rowing and travelling long distances across the waters to trade, mate, marry, and celebrate their abundance and existence.

In Paia, I watch the weather change dramatically and swiftly, from sunny to windy, to too-rainy-to-see-through and back again to too-bright-with-rainbows. Here, I think about the Seven Archetypes, dreaming, rationing, and reasoning about how best to communicate these beliefs that stir within me.

As I sit under one of the varied species of palm trees, many brought by settlers via wind and sail, I hear the sound of the island, the sound of the wind, the buzz of a bee, the human race's barometer on earth. I prepare myself to meditate on the Sound of the universe. I think of libraries, filled with their volumes of books and the words and wisdom of the world. What books were lost in the destruction of the Library of Alexandria? Did any contain the knowledge of the seven days of the week, their ruling planets and associated Gods and Goddesses? Did any contain the gnosis of the Sound of the universe? Did any contain information about the Time Before Time? What if I could spend a day there reading, researching, learning, and satisfying my soul's search for ancient gnosis? Would I learn how much has changed?

When I look down the streets of Paia, I understand what is meant by the saying, "Change is the only constant."

Wandering the health food and watersports shops of Paia, I encounter people from every nation and hear languages I can and cannot identify. In this vortex of beautiful people, healthy people, curious people, I think of the Mercury Archetype and how the movement and flow of energy between us all keeps us aligned to caring for one another and for the Earth.

As I sit sipping a coffee, I begin to buzz with awareness of how movement (and caffeine, stimulation, or the "stoke") is essential to happiness and health. I listen to an eighty-four year old windsurfer describe, with the excitement of a child, how dolphins swam by his side for over a mile. Two women are discussing a tai chi class they attended for the first time and their voices vibrate already with clarity and determination to make this practice by the sea their new life mission.

Sports therapists and nutritionists tell us now daily that the secret to a long life of minimal pain, inflammation, and injury is to keep on moving. Walk, jog, run, hike, swim, dance, climb a rock wall, ski, skate, stretch, take tai chi—whatever we do, we must get out of the chair, get outside, and go. Mercury moves us! We are moved by Mercury psychologically too. When obstacles are set in our way and we stagnate, fall into a rut, or freeze with fear, we can call upon Mercury to push onward. As we move through panic, pain, boredom, or trouble and we grow—we change. We can breathe, focus, function, and have fun again.

Mercury brings new light to the question "Who am I?" because when under Mercury's influence, we are most likely not quite who we were just a few weeks or months ago, and we have not quite fully stepped into the person we will shortly be. This state of limbo is natural and human, and transformation is not always easy, but it is never dull. Wednesday's child is full of woe, full of "Woden." "Woe is me," is the comical and overdramatic way that Mercury communicates their personal interactions as they take a sigh, take in air and breathe. The Mercury Archetype can suffer from "emotional empathy," as they are easily influenced by others and their feelings, and this is their woe. Their behavior is easily affected by the world as a whole, and they tend to learn, know, and feel too much. They carry too much wisdom, intellect, and knowledge. They take that deep breath—that long sigh—in order to catch their breath and silence the woe.

Think of your friends who are "mercurial" by nature—they enter a room and light it up, but by the time they exit that very same room on the very same night, they are inexplicably grouchy. Their moods are unpredictable, but their minds overflow with great ideas and they never run out of them. Like thermometers, they change, hot to cold and cold to hot and everything in between.

They have been all over the world, changed countries, careers, jobs, languages, appearances and even their names. They are the changeling. They tell you all the stories, and I mean *all* the stories. They can be longwinded. They know and tell you all the jokes. They are witty responders. They have the one-liners. They have the facts, the information, the answers, the stats, and the numbers. They changed from being encyclopedias to search engines. They are the Readers Digest and Cliff Notes of our lives. They know the languages and the words. They are adaptable, and can be or can do anything and everything. They can be a one-man-band. They adapt to any circumstance and are easily influenced by family, friends, teachers, or any figures in their lives, therefore they are hard to grasp or get a hold of.

Mercury has thousands of unrelated facts at his/her fingertips, which he can combine at will to impress people. If it becomes obvious that you know more about the subject than he does, he will take the conversation in another direction, often by making a joke. Humor is Mercury's domain and he will use it to shake others out of their comfort zones, or routines and traditions.

The mind is activated bringing a strong sense of ration, reason and intellect, sometimes too much or too many minds or personalities. They are ambidextrous, and are prone to being diagnosed with ADD and ADHD. The consummate multi-tasker, they either get many things done at once or can't accomplish anything at all, as they are juggling too many balls. They can be machine-like, computer-like robots, whom comprehend the language and magic of invention and technology, mechanics, robotics, droids, cyborgs, AI, all things "tele" and all things "comm."

The Mercury Archetype is, like the silver metal itself, alluringly beautiful and dangerously toxic. Inhaling or digesting mercury can damage organs and the nerves. It can cause the skin to crawl, turn pink, and peel; and its effects can sometimes lay dormant for months—and then death becomes inevitable. But Mercury is used to conduct electricity and to mine other rare and valuable metals, such as gold.

Mentally, Mercury rules the internal winds of our moods and emotions. It manifests as instability, inadaptability, impatience and fickleness, as the need to change, to go retrograde, to lie and deceive and the tendency to do too many things at once.

Physically and physiologically, Mercury rules the lungs, respiratory system, breath, equilibrium, our hearing and ears, our speech and throat, the tongue, lymph, glands, and bodily temperature changes. Wednesday's children have the capacity to soar like birds. They possess high levels of coordination, speed, and dexterity, and are quick, swift, and alert like winged creatures of the air.

A Mercury Archetype dresses to communicate their personality, which is often witty, vivacious, "jester-like," the joker. Your Mercury friends can be spotted quickly in a large crowd by their red converse shoes (which they have doodled on with Sharpie to pass the time) and two different colored socks. Their cargo shorts are held up with a rainbow colored belt, and on windy days, they wear a flannel shirt full of holes to cover a tattered t-shirt and suspenders. A leather hat with a feather in it protects their overly busy head from sunburn and their glasses are crooked and bent and taped on one side. They might smoke a cigarette, leaving behind a heady scent of tobacco and yesterday's sweat. Wednesday's child is a mix-matched chameleon of unmatched unpredictability and instability. Or they can dress the opposite, as the perfectly aligned for the occasion chameleon. Each day of the week they might wear a different sports team logo, a different color, or a different style. Multi-faceted in all regards, the Mercury Archetype reminds me of Paia town.

On quiet mornings in Paia, when the wind is not yet roaring, you catch sight of a Mercury Archetype winding her way down the sidewalk in flowing fabrics of mixed patterns. You hear nothing but sugar cane blowing in the breeze and an occasional coconut falling to Earth. Waves crash nearby, and on rare occasions, you hear someone blowing a conch shell in the distance or someone spreading gossip via the "coconut express," the island style of communicating. As the town wakes up, the static begins, and the people in Paia begin to buzz with the need to connect. This is the time when I simply remember what my mom taught me as a child about the importance of air and breath, the need to breathe and slow down. She taught me this lesson — to breathe in slowly through one's nose, first from the belly and then into the lungs and out through the mouth releasing all tension.

Whichever of the only two types of winds that blow through Paia is blowing—either the trades from the west, or the Konas from the east—people do not sit still in Paia unless they are meditating. This town is the changeling. Vans loaded with surfboards pass by, bearing worldly bumper stickers that read: "London, Paris, Tokyo, Paia." Buses, bicyclists, skateboarders whirl and whizz along. And yet as much as everyone is on the move, is fit, is active and engaged. Paia, like Mercury, is in retrograde. It's a place that appears to be receding and misdirected.

This retrograde is, of course, an optical illusion; it is an effect of the planet Mercury's speed.

Do you ever wonder which bird gets to be the lead bird, gets to set the pace and direction? Which bird is chosen to communicate with God, the Source of All, the universe, the flow, the stream, the Sound? Do you ever wonder which human being gets to be the "First Scribe of God?" Which human is chosen to be the communicator with God, our Creator? What does it take to communicate with that knowledge? Mercury helps.

The Mercury Archetype goes through life with what I like to call the "Mercury Breath, Conscious Mind and Intellect of the Communicator" with the lungs and respiratory system activated and the Power to "Communicate." When the Mercury Archetype "has air" and the lungs and respiratory system are strong, this archetype has an incredible capability to communicate. They are sound in their conscious mind, and can regulate their intellect, intelligence, ration, and reason. They adeptly master science, technology, and computers, and they show coordination, dexterity, speed, reactivity, sensitivity, and adaptability.

When the Mercury Archetype does not have air and the lungs and respiratory system are weak, they lack breath and communicate with measurably less force and effectiveness, or without truth, shifty and shady.

Mercury gives us facility of congealing, mesmerizing, moving, flowing, and taking the pulse of the temperature in any room. At their best, Mercury Archetypes walk into a board meeting or a party full of strangers and bring people together. Their adeptness with words and language helps "translate" conflicting opinions and beliefs, and results in harmony and consensus. They are the middle man and middle woman, either or, or both, the hermaphrodite. In the presence of a Mercury Archetype that is on top of their game, people from all walks of life feel heard, valued, and respected.

At their worst, the Mercury Archetype sucks up all the air in the room. Their jumpiness spreads like the aftershocks of an earthquake, and renders everyone "on edge" or anxious. Unless someone reminds them to inhale and exhale, deeply, they might start five projects all at once, in one hour, and follow through on nothing by the end of the day, month, or year.

The colleague who comes to work talking about their model train, which runs through a model town that takes up the entire basement of their house, might be a Wednesday's child. Anything to do with transport, buses, trams, cars, trains, roads, railways, the post office, couriers, letters, parcels, mobile phones, phones, agents, agencies, shops, bartering, buying/selling, craftsmen, manual dexterity, and writing implements—this is the terrain Mercury.

Writers, poets, journalists, teachers, and those who manage schools, transportation systems, trade, and commerce—your wheelers and dealers, your spin doctors and your stealers—lawyers and negotiators, these are Mercury's people.

A master with words, communication, and writing, they work with their feathers and quills, their pens and pencils, their papyrus and paper, their journals and their computers, tablets, and phones, using whatever it takes to spread the word.

They are lingual, bi-lingual, and multi-lingual. They communicate, speak, and interpret with many voices, tones, and octaves. They hear from their larger or extraordinary ears. They search out and find things and activities to stimulate their lungs, exploring breathing and breathing techniques, running and swimming, and even smoking and inhaling vapor.

On the positive side, Wednesday's children are quick-thinking, curious, and expressive. They bring people and ideas together, and can be rational and lighthearted at the same time. They adapt well anywhere, with anyone. They are just at ease when talking to a rodeo clown as they are engaging with a CEO or president of a large corporation.

When they are not on top of their game though, those under Mercury's influence tend to be shallow, glib, slick, artful, sly, and nosey. Like those seabirds on the wires in Paia, they chatter and gossip, they are flighty, easily influenced and distracted. If they take their rationalizing too far, they stop feeling, which interferes with their usual ability to communicate.

The jittery person sitting next to you at the café, the one shaking his leg and rattling the table, this is a Mercury Archetype under duress—never settling, nervous, inconsistent, and scattered. In their mind, they are likely splitting hairs and being self-critical.

The struggle in balancing, for Wednesday's child, involves acknowledging one's speed and agility. Being taken by the wind is both a good and a bad thing, but when the wing-footed messenger slows down and takes in their surroundings, clever conquers dull and free wins over fussy. Consciously toning down all that is hyper—one's hyperactivity or hypersensitivity—helps tame the mercurial nature of the Mercury Archetype. When too many words are coming in or out too fast, intellect and intelligence cannot function. Acknowledging external influences, experiencing them, and then letting them go, helps overwhelmed Mercury Archetypes to speak, write, and make themselves clear. Let's investigate the Mercury Archetype further.

1. The Seven Days of Creation and of the Week

In our seven-day creation story, on our fourth day of creation—Wednesday—God provides a way to mark what is sacred. Time flows and seasons change. Just as these cycles continually roll in the backdrop of our lives, we actively meditate on the meaning of Mercury and Wednesday, and we greet and accept all changes we must face and lean into. If the universe is constantly changing, so can we—so must we. This is growth, and growth is good. We celebrate change and aging with each birthday, and in smaller ways throughout the year.

The "vault of the sky," or the Above consisting of the sky, the heavens, and all the stars and planets (or "planetos") can be seen as the air clears. Mercury, the hermaphrodite planet of air and wind, of both sides, of light and dark, and of sun and moon, is represented as the in-between that sets the scientific stage of the Cosmos. The fourth day of creation, like Mercury, says so much, and yet at the same time, so little, perhaps to mislead and confuse us, as Mercury often does.

Wednesday is commonly referred to—to the joy of many pre-teens—as "Hump Day," and many people consider it the "turning point" or pivot of the traditional workweek, where we can see the light at the end of the tunnel, in the form of the upcoming weekend. It is the middle, the middle man, and the messenger of the week.

2. The Seven Naked Eye Planets

Although we can all think of Mercury, only some of us can think like Mercury. The first-century poet Manilius described Mercury as an inconstant, vivacious, and curious planet. Being the smallest planet and closest to the sun, it is difficult for spacecraft to visit. It is the most pockmarked—or cratered—planet, and it is also wrinkled. Mercury has no moons and is only slightly larger than the Earth's moon. The speedy little planet makes its way around the sun in just eighty-eight days. The first NASA spacecraft to orbit Mercury was aptly named MESSENGER.

The planet Mercury is a hyper, reactive, mutable, and variable planet, as is the Mercury Archetype. The planet is known for going into retrograde, or appearing to slow down as other planets catch up and pass it by. But this is a trick, a deception, and an illusion of the conscious mind, and the God Mercury is the ruler of tricks and deception.

3. The Gods of Myth

Mercury, also known as Hermes (Greek), Mercury (Roman), Woden (Norse), Thoth, Hermes Trismegistus and Buddha, is the Messenger God, the God

116

of communication, commerce, intellect, ration and reason, language and learning, science and technology, travel and speed.

As a baby, Hermes, son of Zeus and Pleiad Maia, and the messenger God of travel, commerce, communication, thieves, and trickery couldn't stay or sit still. One day, bored, he impulsively left his crib and set out to steal his half-brother, Apollo's, cattle. To escape and get his loot into hiding, Hermes attempted to confuse anyone tracking him (namely Apollo, the God of Prophesy) by attaching his shoes and the cattle's hooves in reverse. But brothers being brothers, Apollo of course knew what Hermes had done. He finds him and brings him to Zeus to be judged.

Hermes, who has a way with words, first lies, but then confesses the truth. Zeus is amused and rather than punishing Hermes, asks him to return the herd to Apollo. Hermes, feeling remorseful, offers Apollo a handcrafted tortoiseshell lyre and realizes honesty is the best policy. Who knows if he, or any of us will always stick to the best policy, but clearly when we do, we are stepping into our highest communicator or messenger selves. The character in our lives who says "honestly" and "to tell the truth" all of the time—are they being honest now? Are they always honest? Do they speak with so much honesty that they must constantly draw attention to it? So, the state of retrograde in communication is confusing—it says so much, or does it?

The Mercury Archetype dwells under the spell of Mercury, or Hermes. When conjuring this God, you bring on change, often more rapidly than usual. Mercury is as hard to grab hold of as quicksilver. He moves things around, and not always with permission (think of those mischievous children you know, or thieves). As the alchemists know, he changes forms that have become stabilized, and movement without form is his ideal.

4. The Archangels or Guardian Angels

Raphael is most frequently called upon for help in finding the right path. If your health, emotions, or spirits are out of whack, he cuts through the static and shows you the practical, no-nonsense way toward growth. He is the angel of healing and wisdom, and is also a source of tools for self-improvement and self-enrichment. Raphael, like Mercury, is a lover of learning and learners. In art and literature, this angel is usually depicted carrying a caduceus, the very same Staff of Hermes Trismegistus, an instrument that he uses to heal and to put anyone who needs him in contact with the divine, the spiritual, the universe.

5. The Seven Classical Metals

Mercury exists—like Hermes Trismegistus, who was "thrice born"— in three states: liquid, solid, and vapor. In its liquid state, it weighs 13.6 times more than water, and if spilled, forms back to its original state again quickly. No wonder mercury is associated with changeability that is at times almost imperceptible.

Mercury can be dangerous and lethal, in any of its states, and in various degrees of ingestion, inhalation, or contact. Mercury easily influences and causes reactivity. The fish we eat can be a source of mercury, and of mercury poisoning. We release mercury into the environment when we burn coal and mine gold. Symptoms of mercury poisoning include skin rashes, anxiety, and difficulty seeing, hearing and speaking. The famous "Mad Hatter" became "mad," or crazy, thanks to the mercury nitrate he used in the craft of making felt hats. People die of mercury poisoning, sometimes months after they have had contact with the metal.

But of course, we rely on mercury as a conduit of electricity and to draw out other metals, such as gold. We use it in barometers, to measure air pressure and changes in the weather, so that we may better plan our days and nights, our travels and adventures.

6. The Seven Vortexes, or Chakras and Organ Systems

The fourth vortex, which is the "air," "the breath" or "the chest" chakra, represents Mercury. Physically and physiologically, this is the vortex that spins and hums primarily for the Mercury Archetype, and it regulates our lungs, our in and out breath, the respiratory system, our nerves, glands, communication, intellect, and coordination. When we activate this vortex, we stimulate the conscious mind and our lungs, and we lighten up and brighten up. We fill ourselves to capacity and we release and let go of what we do not need.

When our ability to breathe is diminished or our Mercury system is being attacked—either by particles in the environment, asthma, allergies, illness or stress—our natural ability to move and go with the flow, is hampered. We stiffen up, our shoulders move toward our earlobes, and we cannot communicate as effectively as we normally can, or should. Slowing down and paying attention to breathing is the best way to appease an overactive Mercury influence. Meditation and yoga masters have used breathing as a path to wellbeing and balance for centuries, and scientists of all stripes are today proving the value of breathing—which should come naturally, but often has to be consciously practiced—on mental health and happiness. Breathe air, one of the building blocks of life, into the belly, like Buddha. Breathe into the belly, lungs, throat, nose, and mind—and let go.

7. Planetary Age and Hours Cycles

From ages seven to fourteen, we are in our Mercury years. During this time, we are coming out of our initial unconscious and subconscious years of sleep and dreams, and into our rational mind. We begin now to test out and to practice reason. In our Mercury years, we grab command of our language and communication skills, which we use to navigate the universe as social beings. Via words and numbers, we dig in at school, accepting guidance from our teachers. We carry our books, pens, pencils and papers, compasses, erasers, notebooks, and, of course now, our laptops, tablets, and phones. In our leisure time, we read the books we choose and begin travelling further through imagined worlds. We also begin travelling to and from school, and possibly to other states and countries, with an awareness of what this travel brings.

Finally, we get to play board games that are labeled "Ages 7 and up," as well as logic, strategy, and rational games like checkers and chess. Our teachers stimulate our curiosity by requiring us to collaborate in small groups on lab work, or to construct and build models and science projects.

These are also our adaptive or expansive "lung years" in which we ask a thousand questions: How does this work? What does that mean? Why? Why? These are the years in which our interests "mature" and change, and our bodies morph from child to young adult. These are the years that I got my first Curious George lunchbox.

The Mercury Planetary Hour is from 3:26 a.m. to 6:52 a.m., the time in which we complete our deep sleep, show restlessness and then become awake and aware in the world around us. The Ancients considered this planetary hour the "double" planetary hour in which the ruling planet of the day of the week is the same, or twin, of the planetary hour. Everyone born in this planetary hour is a "double" Planetary Archetype (See Planetary Archetype Chart) and has the same planet ruling their major/primary and minor/secondary archetype, and with this comes the double blessings and gifts as well as the double malediction and curse.

8. The Seven Lost Symbols

Mercury's symbol, ☿, is the symbol of Wednesday, and the ruler of Wednesday's child and the Mercury Archetype. Mercury is represented by the head, winged cap, ears and Caduceus of Hermes Trismegistus and of the God Mercury, Hermes or Woden.

9. The Twelve Sun Signs of Contemporary Astrology

Up/down, left/right, west/east, north/south, ahead/behind, hot/cold, above/below, here/over there, over there/here, back/forth, top/bottom—the Mercury Archetype represents duality more than any other Archetype there is. Gemini and Virgo are the corresponding sun signs.

Like Gemini, Mercury Archetypes can be fast talkers and amazing multi-taskers. Though your Mercury friend might sometimes appear to be "spacing out" during a conversation, they are actually pulling together multiple threads of what is being said, and because of this ability, they are especially adept at building teams that gel well together. They excel at "cross-cultural" or "cross-department" communication building. They excel at containing dual, many, or cross-personalities all at once. The Twins the hermaphrodite, and Geminis are ruled by Mercury.

Just as Gemini loves to bounce around from idea to idea and from project to project, so too, does the Mercury Archetype. Routine can help these people focus, but beware of Mercury's kryptonite—restlessness and boredom!

Geminis are known as "everybody's best friend," because they can talk on virtually any subject with either deep enthusiasm, genuine knowledge, or feigned interest. Ruled by the wind, they can turn easily from the life of the party into a windbag, so again, dear Wednesday's Child, take a deep breath to restore balance and prevent constantly blowing other people's socks off.

Virgos can be so critical, picky, opinionated, practical, logical, mutable, and restless that they cannot find balance. They can't sit or stay still; they need to move, run, travel, change, adapt, and mutate. Virgos are the curious whiz kids, the intellectuals, the intelligent ones. They are the rational and reasonable ones, the logical ones, and they need to know, to understand, and to comprehend.

If you are a Mercury Archetype, reading about Gemini's and Virgo's strengths and weaknesses, desires and distastes, will help lead you to answers to the question "Who am I?"

In Conclusion

The more the Mercury Archetype learns about Mercury as a celestial body and the more we understand and believe in all its associated Gods and Goddesses, the more we can learn to balance our in-breath with our out-breath, our taking with our giving, and our urge to fill silence with talk.

One of the most important aspects of the Mercury Archetype is change and adaptability. In fact, they are so adaptable that we must look at their minor, or secondary, planetary archetype more than any of the other archetypes (See Planetary Archetype Chart), to fully understand them. Although we each have a minor planetary archetype, and a secondary influence, (Mercury is my minor planetary archetype) it is the Mercury Archetype that is most influenced, changed, or adapted to that planet's traits, qualities and attributes.

The Mercury Archetype goes through life as the God of travel, trade, communication, the intellectual mind and wisdom. Complex ideas and beliefs can be broken down and brought to the layperson, or to the masses, by Wednesday's children. Have information that needs to be quickly assimilated and dispersed—get your Mercury Archetype on it! See a friend or colleague that is struggling with any of the typical Mercurial "weaknesses," i.e. indecisiveness, changeability, or instability? Offer to take a brisk walk with them outdoors for a breath of fresh air.

The Mercury Archetype represents our active intelligence, the ability to reason and ration, critically think, analyze, and understand. They learn, teach, educate, and ignite our mental faculties.

The Mercury Archetype makes jokes, plays tricks, and cannot hide their quirks. They are the authors, writers, entertainers, actors, comedians and singers amongst us, and if they aren't completely jet set, they surely are not your couch potatoes. They go through life not as a metal, a solid, a liquid, or smoke, but are all forms, simultaneously. They are on the edge of their nerves and get on our nerves. So motley, they can be and do anything. They are not communicators for communication's sake. They connect the dots via words, travel, trade and commerce, science and technology, and medicine. They are great at athletics with dexterity, balance and intellect and musicians (although they may play their instrument backwards or upside down, playing and singing to their own tune).

Mercury is the hermaphrodite God and Goddess, the communicator, the in-between, and the thermometer. Mercury Archetypes are edgy and on edge, flighty and flippant. They are silver-tongued, sometimes to the point of being deceptive. But above all, they are influential, walking on air and always able to capture the ears and minds of those around them.

CHAPTER TWELVE

THE JUPITER ARCHETYPE

And God said, "Let the water teem with living creatures, and let birds fly above the earth across the vault of the sky." So God created the great creatures of the sea and every living thing with which the water teems and that moves about in it, according to their kinds, and every winged bird according to its kind. And God saw that it was good. God blessed them and said, "Be fruitful and increase in number and fill the water in the seas, and let the birds increase on the earth." And there was evening, and there was morning—the fifth day.

—Genesis

THURSDAY, 5:10 P.M. – 8:36 P.M.

HANA IS MOST DEFINITELY A PLACE OF GOD, A PLACE OF HEAVEN ON EARTH. It is a place of abundance, blessings, and prosperity. The environment is respected here; it is tended, worshipped, and nurtured. In turn, this place provides nourishment, energy, refuge, and beauty. Hana, for me is my fifth seven wonder on Maui and the ideal place to "meditate with Jupiter" and to reveal the meaning of Thursday ("Thor's-Day"), the fifth day of creation, the fifth day of the week, and the day of the Jupiter Planetary Archetype.

Breathtaking Wailua Falls is located in the eastern rainforest of Maui, just past Hana Town. Although currently a popular and easily accessible roadside attraction, quietness can still be found by following the short trail that leads to the small pool at the base of the waterfall. There are still hours where one can sit in the blissful mist in solitude, and I do.

It is evening, the time wherever I am, that I take time to sit and reflect back on my day. During this ritual moment, I make a point of acknowledging and being grateful for everything God has blessed me with. On this particular evening in Hana, I sit like I did as a child, by a bountiful fragrant ginger plant. Instead of eating dinner this night, I am fasting, which I do several times throughout the year to allow my digestive fire, my liver, and my metabolic system to rejuvenate. As thunder begins to roll and lightning forms in the distance, my empty stomach and intestines growl and grumble with hunger. All of these sounds—as Above, so below—remind me of the sound of aluminum foil being balled up, or a wobbly metal cooking sheet being placed in the oven.

Thanks to my mother, who was an early student of traditional healing practices and medicines, I learned as a child the importance of diet and nutrition, especially the importance of a whole food, plant based diet with fruits and veges grown from good soil enriched with vitamins and minerals, as well as the use superfoods and herbs. Including in this is the many purposes and benefits of ginger. Whether I am fasting or indulging in my favorite foods, ginger is important to me as a digestive tonic. This plant's aroma takes me directly back to the many hikes I have made in Hana. When I make ginger tea at my current home on the mainland, I only need to close my eyes and inhale, and I am cruising the Hana Highway along the drop-off cliffs, with my windows rolled down, and the sea, sun, and lush jungle infiltrating my senses.

Once you get past the hustle and static of tourists on the infamous hairpin road to Hana, you can find seclusion. Visit one of the waterfalls on a day of thunder and lightning, and chances are, you will find yourself alone with nothing but misty rainbow prisms shimmering overhead. Sitting at one of my favorite locations on this side of Maui, I am reminded of a dream I had as a child, a dream I will never forget.

In that night's travels, I came upon a waterfall, and at the top of the falls, carved in the rocks the waters spilled over with force and grace, I saw the face of God. In his right hand, he held an antique lantern that shone with the Sun as its torch. In his left hand, he held a scepter that was globed at the top as the Moon. God's beard was the flowing water, and floating on top of the pool at God's feet, was a chessboard. On this chessboard, there we were, humans, playing the game of life. As an adult, I now see in this dream, water as the reincarnation of life, energy, and abundance—As Above, so below.

The Jupiter Archetype goes through life with an appetite for many things: God and religion, wealth and money, power and might, and food and drink. God, represented in most all religions and churches, also includes faith, spirituality, the metaphysical, and higher knowledge and learning. The Jupiter Archetype is known to overindulge, which leads it to being known as the God of gods, the Ruler of rulers, the King of kings and the one that brings morals and values, as well as over-righteousness and piousness.

Money, money, money is this archetype's mantra, chant, ritual, and prayer. Wealth, wealth, wealth is the attraction, the attention, the intention. Jupiter is about financial security. Jupiter is the planet, and God, known as the "Great Benefactor" or the benevolent one. This god brings growth, expansion, wealth, abundance, prosperity, and opportunity, or at the very least the search for all of the above. There is no doubt a greedy side to the Jupiter Archetype, and they can be cheap tight hoarders.

As the authority figure, Jupiter is fed by power and might, which they easily attain through government, politics, justice, and moral code making. This archetype struggles to enrich and balance all of humanity through laws and bills, expenses and budgets, taxation and spending.

Food, drink, and merriment, in the Jupiter child's mind, are meant to be consumed. Anything that brings life and sustenance, or security in the form of feeding and fueling the intestinal fire, the liver, the digestive and metabolic systems, as well as our fats and tissues—all of this, is for the taking. Grow, gain weight, lose weight—it is Jupiter, aka, Jolly Jove, who invented the feast, as well as the famine.

My whole life, sitting amongst the trees of Maui, watching the mosquitos and hearing in the distance at times the snorts of feral pigs and the mating calls of mountain goats, led me to becoming a naturalist. I am an environmentalist, a conservationist, a worshipper of nature and all that God has given us for energy and security: mountain apples, guavas, lilicois, bananas, ferns, and starfruit. On Maui, I think of how the ancient Gods and Goddesses lived off the nectar and ambrosia of the land, the very nectar of the Gods and Goddesses. When I am given the opportunity to pluck my own Godly ginger, fruits or veges for consumption, I remember the golden rule, which is to take only what we need from the land and from God, and never more.

Jupiter expresses and expands in our lives as God, as religion, and as houses of God in the form of churches, chapels, cathedrals, temples, shrines, and monasteries. From the Almighty to the people of God and the church come the elders, priests, prophets, clerics, saints, ministers, pastors, and reverends.

Not only is the church ruled by Jupiter, but, so too, is the state. Being the Law Maker and the Rule Maker is a big job, but it is a perfect fit for the Jupiter Archetype because it allows them to be in power, to bring morals, values, ethics, and ideals to a society.

It is on Maui, surrounded by such an abundance of food, that I am reminded of the Jupiter Archetype's hunger. This archetype must be careful not to overindulge. The liver, metabolic system, gastro-intestinal tract, thyroid, colon, pancreas, fat, and tissues are activated by the gassy giant. When healthy, the digestive fire and the ability to create energy out of foods is strong. When out of balance, there can be too much or not enough growth—the Jupiter Archetype becomes, too fat or too skinny,

Hana is the symbolic town of Jupiter; it is under the influence of Jupiter. In these rainforests, the rains of God bring down to Earth a heavenly mana. This place is tropical, lush, sacred, and teeming with sustenance and life. The vegetation grows as much as the rain pours, and nourishes the body and soul.

Hana is a town of religion, faith, churches, spirituality, enlightenment, and God. This is a town of thunder and lightning, the sounds, light, and voice of Jupiter, Thor and Jove. Nestled in the deepest, darkest greens, in Hana you imagine it is possible that money grows on trees.

From the Holy Roman Empire's Thaler, we got the almighty dollar, the world's standard of wealth, and the most circulated papyrus of our time. From its "In God We Trust" message to the symbolic Bald Eagle of morals, virtue, justice, politics, power, and control through war (the talon and arrows) and peace (the olive branch), the bill holds the Jupiter Archetype's value. The all-seeing "Eye of Providence" tops the familiar pyramid of ages, like the golden globe tops the Caduceus. Does Hermes Trismegistus still watch from behind that eye?

God is not stingy in Hana; God does not hold back here. Here, all is plentiful and ripe for the harvest. Here, Jupiter is God, and he is in charge of wealth, accumulation, prosperity, abundance, expansion, and growth. Jupiter promotes goodwill, humanitarianism, environmentalism, philanthropy, and conservationism. Higher learning and knowledge matter to most of our Gods and Goddesses, and Jupiter is no exception.

The Jupiter Archetype has far to go and far to grow, mentally, emotionally, but also physically. Like the tree that just grows, they too, just grow. They are the gentle and Jolly Green giants with large belly laughs that walk among us, tall and humungous, like great trees. They "live long and prosper." They are large and in charge, hovering above us, looking down upon us, judging us in knowledge and wisdom, in morals and values, in dogma, and in height and weight.

Our tree-like friends can knock us down with a blow of their hand, but can also pick us up. They can judge or give blessings. They can take our money in church—hallelujah—but they also help with charity. They can be redeemed or damned. They may create laws and rules to control, but they protect. They create social programs for doling out money and food. Like the trees, Jupiter Archetypes protect their own in terms of social, economic, religious, national, or political status. When they lack the right "soil," they become stunted, they do not grow—they are small-minded, unlearned, wasteful, greedy scrooges, or atheists.

In Hana, it is hard to imagine the downside of the Jupiter Archetype. Here, waterfalls flow year round. Spiritual wisdom, morals, values, and ideals also flow and accumulate in swirling, refreshing, life-giving pools. The laws of nature and the laws of humankind take seed here, root here, bud and branch out. Where the mighty waterfall crashes thunderously with power and authority, the heavens rain virtues down to Earth.

In Hana, I feel blessed. I see miracles. I lived the miracle here, as a child, in the form of a near death experience, so close to God, to Heaven, to the Above, yet so far to go, as I was given life, or did I chose life and to keep on living in the so below? I pray and give praise. I am thankful for the blessing that we call life, to be human, to stay human and to be humane. Praises to the Almighty! I perform rituals small and large, and take part in or observe ceremonies that were born at the break of dawn, or where the water crests before tumbling from top to bottom.

The Hammer of the Gods, the Hammer of Jupiter (or Thor), the thunderclap, the Hand of God, the Fist of the God of Might, the Hand which controls and commands the weather—you can hear it in the sky. It can startle you with its force, get your attention with a strike of energy, or knock you out with one punch or blow. That is the power that the Jupiter Archetype wields and yields. Climb a tree to touch the sky and bottle lightning, here in Hana.

Thor recently came out of retirement (I would guess so in the search for more financial security) to grace us on the silver screen of Hollywood. It is the Jupiter Archetype that searches out fame and fortune, power and influence. It should come as no surprise that many chase their dreams in Hollywood, but do we need to be reminded that the Academy Awards are made of gold-plated Brittanium, an alloy that is 93% tin, Jupiter's metal?

Hana is as far from Hollywood as you can get, perhaps that is why so many stars come here to just get away. It is far from Waikiki. Here is where I go to find God, to meditate, to restore my faith. Hana is my bountiful rainforest, my religion, my righteousness and my heaven. I expand my horizons here, and grow spiritually, through higher knowledge and wisdom. Being isolated here as a child, even from the small population of Hana itself, I had all the time in the world to climb trees. From my perch, I saw our planet. I ate directly from the trees: breadfruit, bananas, mangos, coconuts, guavas—all of it, any of it.

When I wasn't hanging out above ground in the branches and eating fruit like a half-boy half-monkey, I spent countless hours on our property's fern grotto by the sea. Here, birds flew overhead and we found bounty in the sea. Nearby, an estuary brought the life and food of land, of, fresh and ocean water. We crouched over a pool of water between rocks watching marine mollusks, sea urchins, and crustaceans sway with the incoming and outgoing tides. We caught and ate fish. We lived off the "fat of the land."

The Hana years were the only years I lived without electricity and just the use of a generator as needed. Many decades after mankind learned about the natural energy and power of clouds, thunder, and lightning via the kite and key, the ability to harness electricity in a bulb and spread it out throughout the world via currents, we lived like our ancestors. My family woke to natural light and began to shut our internal energy systems down after the sun dipped beneath the horizon. Without wires overhead and light bulbs to illuminate every room, we burned candles and lanterns, capturing the might and power of Zeus.

Living in the rainforest, we listened for the thunder and lightning of Zeus to predict the rain. This was the source—this falling water—and it filled our streams, waterfalls, and ponds with mana. Having no running water, we relied on this water of life, which ran from the mountains into the stream that fed our little backyard waterfall, pond, and hand pump well.

We had ducks in Hana, and all sorts of tropical birds visited us daily. My first memories of gathering around the dinner table to feast on a Thanksgiving bird come from this place, and I did not know then what I know now: Thanksgiving is celebrated on Thursday, the day of Jupiter or Zeus. On this day of being thankful for all that we have been given, we often cook and overindulge in food, drink, and merriment. We honor and remember our Thursday God.

When I was a kid, I did not know that the word "Amen" means "it is so," and that speaking the word also summons Amen or Amun, who is the Egyptian equivalent of Jupiter, or Zeus. This little Thursday secret may have been lost, hidden, and forgotten, but here I am breathing it back into the mainstream. We should not forget that we all are guided by the Gods and Goddesses, for they never go too long not thinking about us.

Be blessed about what it is like to go through life with the "Tin Cup and Plate of God and Wealth," the liver and metabolic system activated and the Power of "Growth." When the Tin Cup and Plate are "blessed" and the liver and metabolic systems are strong, the Jupiter Archetype has a healthy liver and metabolic system and the capacity for Growth. They experience development, benevolence, luck, faith, charity, wealth, and accumulation. When the Tin Cup and Plate are "hallowed" and the liver and metabolic system is weak, the Jupiter Archetype has an unhealthy liver and metabolic system and the debility of Growth.

Who are you if you are a Jupiter Archetype? Let's explore.

1. The Seven Days of Creation and of the Week

Looking at our seven-day creation story, and at our fifth day of creation—our Thursday—we see in Genesis water flowing full of life. We are water; we give life. Thursday's Child, like water, has far to go. And when Thursday's Children understand the power and energy they contain and can master, they understand that they can go to the ends of the Earth if they try. Jupiter Archetypes spill over the edges of the Earth like waterfalls. They can move mountains, carve passageways for others to follow, and cleanse and heal us to the core. It is from the water, the water of life, that life was formed on the fifth day. All living creatures of land and sea were created, and were fruitful and multiplied. They brought forth more life, forming the food and sustenance that was necessary for the survival of the human race. It is no wonder we celebrate Thanksgiving on Thursday.

2. The Seven Naked Eye Planets

Although we can all praise Jupiter, only some of us have the praises of Jupiter. Jupiter, the gassy giant, is three hundred times larger than Earth. Many of its "official" sixty-plus moons are larger than planets. Jupiter is of course, associated with growth, accumulation, and abundance. The "Great Red Spot" on its surface, first discovered by Giovanni Cassini in the 17th Century, is a giant (but shrinking) storm of thunder and lightning. Even though Jupiter does not have enough mass to ever become a star, it is known as the "Lucky Star;" so if you are hoping to create wealth and abundance, luck and prosperity, close your eyes and bring to mind this planet—or step outside, look up, and say a little prayer to it. The magnetic field of this planet is large, intense, and born of electric currents. It can attract whatever one wishes—what more do you need to convince you of the power it wields over those born under its spell?

3. The Gods of Myth

Jupiter, also known as Zeus (Greek), Jupiter (Roman) Thor (Norse), Jove, Amen and Amun is the God of religions and faith, the spiritual and meta-physical, higher knowledge and learning, laws and rules, morals and values, might and authority, and power and politics. Overthrowing the Titan Cronus and taking charge of the universe took strategy, planning, perseverance, and luck! When mighty Zeus (aka Jupiter) and his brothers dethroned Father Time, all was chaos, all was unsettled—for a spell. Change is always shaky, but then everyone settles into their respective roles and balance is restored.

Jupiter, becoming the God of all Gods and mankind, held the giant hammer of law and order. As the supreme judge of good and bad behavior, he rewarded those who exhibited the former, and punished those who engaged in the latter. The feasts he threw were over the top, and many a God, a Goddess, and a mere mortal overindulged. When Jupiter woke up from these parties, perhaps hungover, gassy, and a little grumpy, he was said to sometimes turn pious and self-righteous. Some say his remorse and holier-than-thou bilious attitude led him to flood the earth—he does rule the thunder, lighting, clouds, and rain waters—and destroy humankind.

Helping him in his position of seeing all and ruling all from above was his golden eagle. This bird, with its impressive and intimidating wingspan of up to eight feet, accompanied him in rituals that entailed the interpretation of omens, and became a symbol of the Holy Roman Empire. Tossing an occasional lightning bolt to Earth also did wonders to keep mere mortals in line!

4. The Archangels or Guardian Angels

Do bankers have angels? Yes, they do. Thursday's angel is Sachiel, a powerful being, and he is the ruler of money, success, achievement, risk-taking (the kind that leads to success and wealth and finance), abundance, and charity. In art, he is often represented wearing thick flowing bejeweled robes, or standing beneath a "downpour" of coins. The gamblers in Vegas who are moving their lips in prayer are most likely evoking Sachiel. Majesty, prestige, righteousness and respect, business, entrepreneurship, and investment fall from the Above to the below by this Angel.

5. The Seven Classical Metals

Tin is the metal associated with Jupiter. It is soft, yet resistant to corrosion. Tin is slang for money and Jupiter is all about the money. I have seen the Jupiter Archetype attracted to tin and the qualities and likeness of tin: They are attracted to tin cans of food and drink, as well as to tin foil, for the storage of food. Since we don't generally wear tin, nor is it commonly used in jewelry, the Jupiter Archetype finds their riches and richness in all of the precious metals, especially in gold and diamonds. They also might wear their cross, their holy books, or their prayer beads and rosary.

In terms of money (or "tin"), they can be either benevolent or cheap with their savings account, their cash, their wallets, their money clip, and their purses. I see Thursday's Children tithing into those tin collection plates more than anyone else at church, or the least. Tin is a tropical rainforest metal and is used in certain fertilizers to grow food.

6. The Seven Vortexes, or Chakras and Organ Systems

The fifth vortex is the "solar plexus vortex." When we gaze at our navel, we gaze at and from the Jupiter chakra—so daydream on, escape reality every now and then, dream big!

When we process our food, we use Jupiter's "digestive fire." Yes, Jupiter is the gassy planet, and yes, sometimes gas is a part of digestion. Remember, Jupiter is the ruler of abundance and expansion, and when we overeat, we over-stress this chakra and feel the heat, or the pain, of too much chaos in the gut. Physically and physiologically, Jupiter rules the liver, the metabolic system, the appetite, the intestines, the gastro-intestinal tract—all of these barometers of what we are fueling ourselves with—or fooling and self-medicating ourselves with in terms of excess food and drink—fall under Jupiter's reign.

On the other side of the equation, most of us like to call upon the power of Jupiter and this fifth chakra when trying to manifest abundance and expansion of our cash stores and cash flow. Faith spins and hums in our abdomen and when in good balance, our intestinal fire burns at just the right temperature, resulting in spiritual and personal growth, as well as all that keeps us warm and comfortable.

7. Planetary Age and Hours Cycles

From ages forty-nine to fifty-six we are in our Jupiter years, or what Steiner called a "higher state" in terms of knowledge and learning. In this time period, the ego subsides and wisdom steps onto the stage. Life is in full swing as benefits and returns from all we have invested in our families and businesses begin to pay off. In this stage of life, we start to plan for retirement—do we have enough money in the coffers? We, like squirrels, start to hoard for the winter of our lives. We hope too for a little luck. Our investments will pay off or we may even win the lottery.

The planetary hour of Jupiter is from 5:10 p.m. to 8:36 p.m. At this time, many of us are satiating ourselves around the dinner table. We are saying grace, sending up a prayer, and blessing our food and our families. Amen. Those of us who can, or those who want to throw a little celebratory toast Jupiter's way—in honor of the feasts he once hosted—might indulge in "Happy Hour," which could also be called "Jolly" or "Jove" hour.

8. The Seven Lost Symbols

The symbol of Jupiter is, $\mathcal{2}$, consists of the crescent with a horizontal line, or the "Z," or lightning bolt, of Zeus, as well as the "z" of zeta, which holds the value of seven and represents knowledge attained through growth and manifestation. It is also said to represent authority, security, idealism, and good luck (the original horseshoe). The symbol represents the eagle, Zeus' bird, the bird that symbolizes power and connection to the divine, as they soar highest and closest to God, our Creator. This symbol is the ruler of Thursday, Thursday's child, and the Jupiter Archetype.

9. The Twelve Sun Signs of Contemporary Astrology

The Sun Signs associated with Thursday's Child, or with the Jupiter Archetype, are Sagittarius and Pisces. Jupiter rules justice, morals, and values, and he meters out good luck, prosperity, and wealth.

Just as Sagittarians and Pisceans make good missionaries, clergy, preachers, pastors, and ministers, so to do Thursday's Children. Know someone whose intuition always proves right, or someone who is often referred to as a mentor, a mystic, or a guru? Chances are, they are ruled by Jupiter. These people are theologians that excel at leading and performing rituals.

Sagittarius tells the truth, sometimes bluntly—so too does the Jupiter Archetype, who always aims for justice and fairness. Sagittarius, the sage, carries and shares wisdom and knowledge—as teachers, they expand their sphere of influence. They are generous and optimistic. They attract wealth and prosperity, and are blessed with luck and chance. The Jupiter Archetype has good fortune, possibly due to their strong religious, philosophical, moral and philanthropic belief systems.

Pisces, the two fish or the double blessing, represents the growth and abundance of all animals and plants on earth. Jovial and merry, thankful, blessed, and fortunate, Pisces can be devoted to charity and generosity to others. They are deep thinkers with a mind for higher knowledge, understanding, learning, education, morals, values, and ethics. They believe in the miracle, the spiritual, the metaphysical, and the mystical, as Jupiter Archetypes do.

Pisces is highly observant, like Jupiter, who rules from above and oversees all. And just as Sagittarius and Pisces will run for the hills as soon as anyone tries to control them—freedom is *not* "just another word" for people born under these signs—Jupiter Archetypes will bolt (like lighting) the second you start bossing them around and fly like an eagle onto their next learning experience.

Jupiter gives us the gift of government, in all its complexity. This planet, this God, and this archetype are at the root of any society's morals, values, humanity, and laws.

At their best, Jupiter Archetypes listen carefully, take everything into account, weigh and balance all options, and lead with the big picture and the general consensus in mind. When they are off balance or out of sorts, their judgmental attitude makes them difficult to be around.

If you are a Jupiter Archetype, studying up on Sagittarian and Piscean traits will help lead you to answers to the question "Who am I?"

In Conclusion

Jupiter is the Spiritual and Financial Guru of growth, expansion, wealth, accumulation, benevolence, luck, religion and faith. Like the old wise man's beard, the wrinkle of a mystics eye, the Godfather, the Jolly Green Giant, Santa Claus and the tall tree. They live to go far, to live long and prosper, to have knowledge and wisdom. Like the large, dark green elephant ears of tarot, the Jupiter Archetype, like the elephant, holds a deeper meaning and insight, a metaphysical meaning, a spiritual meaning, a larger more important meaning about life. They live for higher levels of ethics and ideals and morals and values and justice of the eagle. They live to be generous, optimistic and benevolent and to preserve, expand and elevate. But be careful, not to overdo and over indulge, as this brings greed, insecurity, righteousness, piety and overeating and gluttony

They live with their appetite for food and drink, stimulating the liver, just as their vortex, or chakra, stimulates the liver. The thyroid and the pancreas, their fats, tissues, abdomen, pancreas, navel, sugars, blood sugar are in turn stimulated. Gas, bloating, indigestion, their weight gain and loss in the hips and thighs

The Jupiter Archetype goes through life as the God of Faith, accumulation, prosperity and appetite - associated with the principles of growth, expansion, prosperity and good fortune; and a person's inner sense of justice and morality and their ideals and higher goals. Jupiter governs long distance and foreign travel, higher education, religion and the law. It is also associated with the urge for freedom and exploration, humanitarian and protecting roles, merrymaking or joviality. Jupiter has rulership over the liver, the metabolic system, the Gastro-Intestinal tract, thyroid, colon, pancreas, fat and tissues. The Jupiter Archetype is full of God, Faith, Spiritual Wisdom, morals, values, ethics, security, wealth, money, finances, luck, fortune, opportunity, growth, expansion, accumulation, generosity, humanitarianism, environmentalism, philanthropy, activism, food and appetite. The negative side is greed, over indulgence and piety.

The Romans held countless festivals of wine dedicated to Jupiter, and when wine is enjoyed in healthy doses for what it is—a living thing and an elixir of truth—all is joyous and peaceful. If celebrated in excess, beware the Red Storm, the indigestion, the "mean drunk" side of Jupiter.

The more the Jupiter Archetype learns about Jupiter as a celestial body and the more we understand and believe in all its associated Gods and Goddesses, the more we can live according to its best tendencies and qualities. Being the "giant" is not always easy: At first glance, Jupiter Archetypes may appear overbearing, they are electric and electrifying, but at their core, they really seek to give everyone their proper space and to put all in order. Order leads to a smooth flowing society. And a smooth flowing society brings about more abundance for all.

Jupiter and his great golden eagle knew how to interpret signs so as to manifest all that was meant to be. A Jupiter Archetype who is open to the natural flow of life, who spreads their wings or their "waters" to the farthest edges of the Earth, and who believes in abundance, receives many blessings.

Each player on the chessboard of life—that chessboard that floats on the pool at the base of the waterfall that is made of the beard of God—understands their role and enthusiastically steps into it.

CHAPTER THIRTEEN

The Venus Archetype

Then God said, "Let us make mankind in our image, in our likeness, so that they may rule over the fish in the sea and the birds in the sky, over the livestock and all the wild animals, and over all the creatures that move along the ground."

So God created mankind in his own image, in the image of God he created them; male and female he created them.

God blessed them and said to them, "Be fruitful and increase in number; fill the earth and subdue it. Rule over the fish in the sea and the birds in the sky and over every living creature that moves on the ground."

God saw all that he had made, and it was very good. And there was evening, and there was morning—the sixth day.

—Genesis

Friday, 6:52 a.m. – 10:18 a.m.

ONELOA, OR MAKENA BEACH, IS ONE OF THE MOST BEAUTIFUL BEACHES on Maui. Being my favorite place on Earth, I might argue it is the most stunning beach in the world. On this lovely pink-hued morning, I sit cross-legged in the evening-cooled sand. The morning tide has left a new line of tiny and broken shells on the shoreline and I stretch my arms, straightening my spine and grounding my sit bones to the Earth.

Gazing skyward, I find Venus, the "morning star." She rises as the sun is just starting to turn all that is rosy and warm, coppery and bright. Gazing oceanward, the Pacific, which means "peace," brings me internal peace, as the foamy waves dance with the sunrise. Makena Beach is my sixth seven wonder on Maui and an ideal place to "meditate with Venus," and to reveal the meaning of Friday ("Friggas-Day")—the sixth day of creation and the sixth day of the week. Here, I welcome the day of the Venus Planetary Archetype.

After working through my own version of the sun salutation—which I think of as my Venus salutation—I walk to another favorite spot on this beach. I find the Kiawe tree I have come to know over the years. This tree is a tropical mesquite, known for its unwelcoming long thorns. One learns to watch their step near the Kiawe, just as one learns to avoid sea urchin spines in rock pools along the ocean shore. But on this particular Kiawe, a small bare "throne" on its horizontal trunk invites me to take a seat.

Mostly alone on Makena Beach, inhaling the salt air, and Venus's wonder, I wonder: Did this species of tree grow such wicked thorns grow to protect this space, Makena, and others like it, from another evasive species—us? Some say that missionaries first planted Kiawe in Hawaii because their long sharp thorns helped "persuade" locals to wear not just sandals to protect their feet, but more clothing to protect their legs, arms, and more "sensitive private parts." These missionaries wanted everyone to cover up their flesh, and to "evolve" out of a primal state of nakedness.

However the Kiawe came here, I appreciate how they bloom with pretty little yellow flowers. These bright blossoms buzz with bees collecting nectar mixed with the harmonious mating calls of birds. These trees, I have learned, reproduce in two ways: First, by spreading seeds, and second, by a process known as "suckering." Kiawe possess a large and shallow root system, like the kidneys, which makes them great in extracting moisture and water. On harsh and dry Makena Beach, all flora and fauna rely on every drop of nourishment they can get to survive. As I take a chug of water, I am reminded of the importance instilled in me by my mother of water and fluids and staying hydrated. With this water I flush the kidneys, bladder, and urinary system. I give life to my skin and hair. I drink water in order to feel and look good and healthy.

Makena, or "Big Beach" Makena, was the first placed my family lived when we arrived on Maui. We camped here, in paradise, before finding a more permanent home, and it is these earliest memories of my off-grid hippie baby upbringing that resonate with all that I do, and all that I am, now.

I was a carefree child of the Earth, ocean, sky, and mountain. I ran naked and exposed down Makena Beach, chasing clouds and rainbows and building sand forts and castles. Unconscious of my nudity and naked state, like Adam and Eve before they ate the beautiful fruit of the Tree of the Knowledge of Good and Evil and their "eyes were opened," I was one with the universe. Going *au naturel* was natural, and there was no shame, modesty, or vanity in it. Pure boy, pure human, I was there for all the Gods and Goddesses to see, all rain to fall on my skin, and all wind to cool or dry me.

We lived, in those days, as pure essence. My mother fed us simply and well, and we treated our Mother Earth as our ancestors treated her millennia ago—with reverence, all in a mutually sustainable give and take relationship.

There is still, near Makena Beach over the sandy hill, "Little Beach," where the free-spirited go to let it all hang out. This swath of sand attracts nudists of all ages, shapes, and sizes. Little Beach is where I first became aware of the naked body beyond my own, or the naked body as a mirror image of Adam or Eve. Watching naked adults walk around, sans fig leaves, I remember as a boy calling men's "things" their "one-eyed sea cucumbers" and women's "things" their "hairy conch shells."

Human sexuality is taboo in many cultures, or at least it is a taboo topic in many childhoods. Even in my easygoing hippie family, I was not given a formal "sex education" until my early teens. So my boyhood curiosity remained just that and I sort of floundered about under the influence of Venus, wondering what the differences between men and women were for, hearing stories about "birds and bees," and then running off in the sand and waves and forgetting about it.

Later, in high school, our class came to Makena Beach to clean it up and keep its pristine beauty alive. Some of us dreamt of bringing a date to the nude beach, but for the most part, we worked on our tans with bathing suits on. We bodysurfed and hung out in small groups to eat, listen to music, and talk about what life might bring us. We wrote the obligatory "most likely to" lists. Whether we loved or hated high school, these were the years of forming some of our best friendships, some which lasted a lifetime, before venturing out into the world to find our way. And then, at night, under the stars and moon, with our "Bacchanalian propensities," we partied. We experimented with drugs, alcohol, and total abandon. We played guitars and danced all night to Bob Marley. In the cover of darkness, our confidence grew and some of us experienced our first kiss on this beach, or more, which is nothing short of myth and magic.

"Aprhros" means "foam," so of course, it was beautiful Aphrodite, aka Venus, who was born from the sea. She is the gift, the Goddess that brings us love, pleasure, beauty, and desire. She rules sex, procreation, nudity, and aphrodisiacs. Because of the apple she "fought for," the mighty Aphrodite symbolizes the apple of many a man's eye, in life and art.

When Aphrodite first reached Olympus, all kinds of hell broke loose. She had multiple affairs, effectively weakening the strongest of the Olympian Gods and mortal men with her overpowering sensuality, affection, and sex. She was a woman who was simultaneously desirable and out of reach, and what drives a person crazier than the unattainable? Who does not love the thrill of the chase?

Everyone fell for Aphrodite. Men wrote songs, poems, and stories about her and for her. Her nude body is painted and represented on thousands of canvases, mosaics, frescoes, and murals. Her every curve and gesture has been sculpted in marble and bronze and then erected in buildings and temples. Anywhere we seek beauty, love, and the capacity to birth more beauty and love, we find her likeness.

Aphrodite, the seductress of many, fell in love with Adonis, the studly hunk. Maybe she saw herself in him and was drawn to his absolute beauty, or possibly she was struck by Cupid's arrow. Who knows for sure, because love and lust are a mystery to most, but the two made quite the pair. I assure you, too, that I have seen this pair in their present form, time and time again. Certain couples just channel and ooze myth. From Aphrodite and Adonis, to Adam and Eve, to Antony and Cleopatra, to Romeo and Juliet, and to Brad and Angelina, man and woman have partnered for friendship, love, marriage, mating, and to test our hearts.

From Adonis, of course, we get the "Bronze Adonis," the "gold," and the "copper standard" of beauty. Fortunately, for mere mortals such as myself, modern-day Adonis figures are rather rare, so the playing field is relatively equal.

Aphrodite/Venus has Greek Goddess Eris to thank, in part, for her trajectory and reputation. When poor Eris was shut out of a party due to her "disagreeable nature," she tossed a golden apple that read "to the fairest" into the air. Party Goddesses Athena, Hera, and Aphrodite all wanted that apple, because who amongst us doesn't want to be considered the fairest, the best looking, the most attractive, or the most beautiful? Countless myths and fables revolve around ego for a reason. As much as I meditate and work on taming my ego, I admit to having a vain streak, or a little bit of Narcissus in my veins.

But back to this battle for the juiciest of apples: Zeus gave Paris, a mortal man, the task of deciding to whom it would go. What a lucky guy!

Here they came, Goddesses Athena, Hera, and Aphrodite, to win him over. Hera offered Paris the gift of power; Athena offered Paris the gift of wisdom; and Aphrodite, well, of course, she offered Paris the love of the most beautiful mortal woman, who she determined was Helen of Troy. How long did it take Paris to make his decision? I do not know, but Helen, who possessed "the face that launched a thousand ships," was the cause of the Trojan War.

Paris tossed that "fairest of them all" apple to Aphrodite and then stole Helen from her husband, a Greek king. Voila—war! Men went to war over the promise of love and the dream of waking up daily to beauty. War is extreme, but who can blame anybody who hopes for such things? Not only do men start wars, but so too, do women, both in the name of love, in the name of the rose, and in the name of beauty, lust and desire, or Venus.

Throughout the ages, from Ancient Egypt, to Antiquity and the Greco-Roman times, to the Middle Ages and into our modern and contemporary age, Venus has been memorialized as the Goddess of love. She is beauty, the lover, the artist, the musician, and the dancer. She is the perfect aesthetic, form, shape, and curve of the human body.

We still see her today as the "Bellas," the beautiful ones who grace us in literature, on TV, and in the movies. From 1980s "coming of age" films to the animated world of princesses and mermaids, we see Venus images and themes. From looking at oneself in the mirror to determine who is "fairest of all," to others being envious and jealous of beauty, to everyone coveting the "beautiful one's" love and affection, or hand in marriage and eternal love, the Venus image overthrows our hearts.

From primitive to modern art, we see Venus. From cave paintings to Playboy and Victoria's Secret, she lives among us, teasing and flirting with her allure and appeal. Fashion and beauty magazines abound—their perfume samples arouse our senses, the smell of Venus, of love and sex. Supermodels rule—their beauty draws us in and we fantasize about becoming them or being with them. Between the pages and between the lines, we read about sex, we devour sexual tips and techniques. We learn how to groom ourselves to attract a mate. We may even read our horoscope in hopes of figuring out our best match and how to win them, All the while, Venus, Aphrodite, Cupid, and Eros are watching us, so below, from the As Above.

What is Venus' or Victoria's secret? What is hidden under the veil when it drops? We all need to be loved and desired. We need to be and feel beautiful and attractive. We wish to be the "model," the artist, the painter, the photographer, or the desired one gazed upon.

In strength, the Venus Archetype oozes the juices of Venus and cries the soft healing tears of Aphrodite. In weakness, this archetype may carry not just the venereal disease of Venus or the physical dysfunction of sex, but also the mental and emotional obstacles of not feeling loved or attractive enough.

The downside to Venus comes from feeling alone—not admired or pursued. The Venus Archetype can sting like a bee, like Cupid's arrow, and can wilt like a rose losing its potency. When down, this archetype must remember that beauty is only skin deep and even a Beast can be beautiful!

The bedroom is the Venus Archetype's domain. They are the seductress under the sheets or in the shower, with aromatic soaps, bath salts, and perfumes. The Venus child can be found looking at their reflection in the mirror throughout the day. Making sure their hair, makeup or clothes are in place, adding another dab of lipstick, brushing a little dog hair off their pants leg—in these small details of appearance, Venus lives and breathes on earth.

Venus, when in the form of Victoria's Secret, is not complete without the rock star—and the rock star is not complete without Venus. Both are under the rule and allure of beauty and music, and both seduce. Rock stars sing the name of their love interest. They croon about how beautiful their beloved looks tonight and about foxy ladies. In assorted love songs and lyrics, we find love, love triangles, exes, cheaters, affairs, flowers, and roses. The rock stars, surrounded by their instruments, are sex symbols. They secrete the sounds and secrets of Venus while surrounded by screaming and gyrating fans and groupies. The Venus Archetypes go hand and hand, like Adam and Eve or any coupled lovers, to give, to receive, and to bond in passion.

The Venus Archetype goes through life with what I call the "Copper Tone of Love, Beauty and the Arts of the Lover" with the kidneys and the reproductive system activated with the power of "Love." When the "tone" of love and beauty is "bronzed," the Venus Archetype thrives. Love and beauty, when appreciated and "warmed" or worshipped, strengthens the kidneys and the reproductive system—and gives us the urge to love (or to make love, which sometimes results in birth). Affection in the form of a big gracious hug, and friendship in the form of guttural laughter and an "all-revealing" comfort and intimacy exist when Venus is in charge and being honored.

Relationships, partnership, sex appeal, art, music, harmony, proportion, diplomacy, peace, and wellbeing belong to the Friday's Child—who is, as the Mother Goose rhyme says, "loving and giving."

Conversely, when our views on love, beauty, and the arts are rusty or corroded, our kidneys suffer, our libido is down, and our ability to reproduce and love wanes.

Venus, as a noun, means "love," or "sexual desire." In Latin, "venerari" means "to please." Venus Archetypes have a mind that needs to be open. They are friendly people who like to please. Friday's Child understands the value of a gift, whether they are giving or receiving one. They are thankful and unafraid to show affection. They are friendly and need their friends. They are sugary sweet and like their sweets. They are like flowers, in looks and smell, and they like their flowers. They are pleasing and like pleasure. They are affectionate and need affection. They like suits and ties and like to tie the knot. They are sensitive—even oversensitive—to touch, taste, pleasure, and of course, love.

Your friend who says, "I love you" all the time, who calls you "friend," or who is known as "the hugger," is likely under the influence of Venus. Most people embrace this friend as happily as he or she embraces them. Hugs, as we know have positive effects on our mental and emotional health. Hugs and kisses, or any human touch, brings happiness to the Venus Archetype. They like massages, manicures and pedicures, their hair being washed and cut, their makeup (or shaving) being done. Bring your Venus Archetypes to all social events to create warmth, comfort, and harmony!

From Phi, we get the golden ration of beauty, the Fibonacci of the world of beauty. This is the perfect size and proportion of the human body that Venus emulated. From "Philo" we get philosophy, or the "love of wisdom," Philadelphia, the city of "brotherly love," and Philanthropist, or a "lover of humans."

Friday's Children are diplomatic, because they are compassionate and need to get along and have peace. They sense what others feel and need, and they spread the wealth—in terms of love, passion, sympathy, and sentiment. Their homes tend to contain art and musical instruments, or they are unique and aesthetically pleasing—reminding you perhaps of the Hanging Gardens of Babylon. The Venus Archetype creates a comfortable abode, a welcome nook, and an inviting garden—where you might find an apple tree. Let's explore the Venus Archetype further.

1. The Seven Days of Creation and of the Week

It is on the sixth day of creation that we see mankind, man and woman, male and female, Adam and Eve created in the image of God—As Above, so below. "Be fruitful and multiply," God said. "Pair and couple together to procreate and replenish the earth, as man and woman, just like the animals." Here, we not only see the first pair of humans, but the duality of creation. We see the first couple, the first partnership, the first marriage, and the first home. And it was good, good like Good Friday, good like Venus and good like God.

It sure seems like God was busy on Friday, trying to get everything done before what we would eventually call "the weekend" came. Reading Genesis, it is as if God knew (and what didn't he know) that Thank God It's Friday would become a mantra. At the end of the traditional workweek, we would all simply want to throw our hands in the air, let our hair down, eat, drink, be merry, and hook up with someone. God gave each animal a mate and asked us to be fruitful! On casual Friday and Friday night, we channel our inner Venus, change from our work clothes to our party clothes, put on a little extra lipstick or don a tie, and we rock out at a concert, attend an art show, or dine at a restaurant with the one we love, under the glow of candlelight. We are social animals and sexual creatures—so bring it on, Friday!

2. The Seven Naked Eye Planets

Although we all might want to be beautiful like Venus, only some of us contain the pure beauty of Venus. Venus is the brightest star in our solar system, and her light literally outshines other stars. Yes, her brilliance attracts the attention, the allure, and the desire of others—and it is not her fault.

I look to Venus, my beautiful love and lover in the sky, my Planetary Archetype, and I think of what life on that planet must be like. Venus is known as the "light bringer," or the phosphorus planet, and I think if only I could walk an hour on her surface, I might achieve a level of clarity and wisdom—about who I am and why we are all here—faster than I can a million lifetimes, anywhere else. Light and love bring us closer to the source of all wisdom and to our purpose, so I meditate on this planet whenever I am feeling particularly alone or lost.

Venus is Earth's "sister," but unlike our watery planet, and like the kidneys that she rules, she has used up all her water and dried up all her oceans. Venus, like Earth's Moon, has phases. Because of these phases, our ancients believed they were seeing two distinct stars, a morning star and an evening star. It was one of my heroes, Galileo, who came by with his wondrous telescope and discovered that Venus was in fact one star, not two.

Venusians, like Martians, exist as a figment of our human imagination. They have been depicted as ghastly spiders, half-gorilla/half-human beasts, or as gigantic frog-like monsters—which given the planet's association with beauty, baffles this human's mind. But of course, each aspect has its opposite, and it is the ugly, unattractive, and hideous side—the beast—which brings about the want and need for the Venus Archetype to feel wanted and loved despite any flaws.

3. The Gods of Myth

Venus is known by many names, Aphrodite (Greek), Venus (Roman), Freya and Frigga (Norse) and Amore, the Goddess of love, marriage, beauty, desire, leisure, entertainment, aesthetics, cosmetics and the fine arts, including literature and writing, painting and sculpting, drawing and architecture, and music and dance. Born of sea foam and carried in a seashell, Aphrodite is the Goddess of balance (she did not tip and fall into the sea, and she becomes a protectress of the sea). Accompanied in art often by Eros and Himeros, or love and desire respectively, she represents all that humankind needs, beyond food and shelter. The cockle shell she rides or rests in, or, that she in some cases holds, symbolizes all that she rules: the divine feminine, human sexuality and fertility, and obviously, female genitalia.

Escorted on her voyages by dolphins and doves, she is the graceful bringer of peace and kindness, a helping hand, though of course, she also had the capacity to spur war. In some depictions, she rides in a flying chariot pulled by swans, and wears a belt that causes everyone to fall in love with her. Aphrodite, or Venus, generates feelings and affections, and the urge to sympathize and unite with others. She is entertainment, and with her soft copper flowing locks and demure but alluring facial expression, she is all we wish to gaze upon.

4. The Archangels or Guardian Angels

Uriel is the angel of the Venus Archetype, and of Friday's Child, the Angel of peace, unconditional love, fidelity, and the Patron of the Arts. Knowing that both good and evil are natural human qualities, and that they often coexist at the same time within the same person, this angel helps those who call upon him to forgive themselves and to move forward with better intentions. Anyone facing a hard choice or experiencing conflict can rely on Uriel to shine light on the lesser of two evils, the right path, or the way toward healthy transformation and growth. This angel is adept at helping mere mortals let go of all that is ailing them or affecting them negatively. Call upon Uriel in times of anguish, especially those involving love and marriage, faithfulness or infidelity, and the need to create peace.

5. The Seven Classical Metals

Copper was mined on the Greek isle of Cyprus, the birthplace of Aphrodite. From these foamy East Mediterranean waters, the Goddess of love and beauty rose. Like Venus, copper is shiny. It grabs your attention and is soft, warm, and malleable; it helps conduct electricity and it bonds and joins things together. It is a friendly metal. Copper, like brass, is found in musical instruments, for example, in horns and cymbals. Most guitar strings are made with copper, and what does music bring to our lives, if not art, love, and beauty? It should come as no surprise to learn that women contain more copper then men, a gift from Venus.

When we sit on the beach and play in the water, most of us will naturally bronze (despite applying sunscreen). The healthy glow we carry home with us from a day outdoors or a week of vacation makes us feel and look more attractive. It may be the Sun that changes our skin tone, but it is Venus that changes the way we feel about our flesh and form. Cosmetics companies understand the value of Venus' copper tinge, and they add copper to their many powders, rouges, and foundations. Flawless skin is a Venus value—one only has to bring Botticelli's *Birth of Venus* or Alexandros of Antioch's Venus de Milo to mind to understand the truth in that statement.

6. The Seven Vortexes, or Chakras and Organ Systems

The sixth vortex, or the "sacral vortex" represents Venus and desire. It is our sexual vortex, and from here we hum and spin love and lust. Passion and pleasure dwell in this chakra, as do all emotions attached to these physical sensations. When this vortex is shining as brightly as it can, much like the planet Venus, it can overtake reason and bring about restlessness. Remember, the Trojan War was initiated by all that comes out of this powerful center. If we dwell here excessively, we may overdo it in terms of our sexuality— we may be promiscuous, perverse or we may become addicted to sex and pornography.

Regulated and managed, of course this chakra brings about the ultimate gift: life! It leads to sex and procreation, and what is more glorious than a mother giving birth to a child? All fantasy, allure, and affections stem from our Venus vortex. All relationships depend on our cultivation of the Venus qualities of tenderness, openness, warmth, comfort, touch, and beauty (not as just a superficial trait, but in the eye of the beholder).

Physically and physiologically, Venus rules our sexual organs, sex drive, and sexual performance which require a healthy-functioning sacral vortex. Water regulation, the bladder, the kidneys, the genital-urinary system, our reproductive system, our ovaries, testes, secretions, veins, sinuses, and mucous membranes require attention to keeping this chakra "hydrated." Beauty is seen in our skin, our hair, nails, lips, and tongue.

7. Planetary Age and Hours Cycles

From age fourteen to twenty-one, we live out our Venus pre-pubescent and puberty years. At this time, we become obsessed with our physical appearance: our skin, our hair, our bodies, and our beauty. We stare, sometimes reluctantly in the mirror, and question our appeal to others. How do I look? Am I beautiful? Am I handsome? Will the object of desire like me, and better yet, will they return my affections?

We wake early in the morning, usually long before our school day begins, to bathe, get dressed, and fix our hair. We look in the mirror multiple times before stepping out the door and we adjust our belt or sweater, we reapply a little makeup, we twist our hair and we dab a little cologne or perfume on our necks and wrists. These are our vainest of years, and we cannot help wanting to be sought out by others. We long for the magnetic appeal of Venus; we believe the apple should be ours. We go to the beach with our friends and don't apply the sunscreen our mothers used to lather on us—we want to be tan, aglow, alive with our youth and our gorgeousness. We develop our first crush and then our first love. We nervously go to our first dance, and then we go for our first kiss. We finally get to watch our first R-rated movies, maybe even X-rated. We lose our virginity. We are physiologically ready to reproduce.

The Venus Planetary Hour is from 6:52 a.m. to 10:18 a.m. During this time, we are rising and performing our morning rituals, making ourselves look as good as possible so that we can seize the day and garner attention. In the "mirror of Venus" we tell ourselves that we are beautiful!

8. The Seven Lost Symbols

When we look at the Symbol, ♀, for Venus, we see the Female and the Feminine, the hand mirror of Venus, the vanity mirror, love and appeal, beauty and balance, marriage and devotion. The Venus Symbol represents the Venus Archetype, Friday's child, the Peace Keeper, the Lover, the Beauty, the Artist, the Musician and love and relationships.

9. The Twelve Sun Signs of Contemporary Astrology

Venus is the evening star and the morning star: she shines as we enter into our darkened bedrooms at night and as we begin to rise in the morning, to face the day. In our bedrooms (or on the beach or in the airplane bathroom!), she oversees all that is associated with seed and receptacle. She is lust, love-making, passion, erotica, sex, whatever you want to call it—and she rules a great part of us, including our most private of body parts.

Like the planet Venus, which is covered in clouds, and like their corresponding Sun Signs Libra and Taurus, Venus Archetypes hide their secrets well. Their main secret concerns sex and sex drive. Because in so many cultures a strong libido is something that is to be regulated or that is relegated to "behind closed doors," this archetype often appears to be winking at you (maybe not literally, but figuratively). Yes, your mischievously flirty friend is likely a Friday's Child. Amused by their own sensuality and sexuality, they are here to remind us all of our own.

Taurus babies and Venus Archetypes have the need for a lover, a partner, or a relationship. They need to be surrounded by beauty and comfort, where they can enjoy in the self-indulgent tendencies of sex, love, pleasure, and sensuality. Taurus, ruled by Venus, indulges in the fine arts and their aesthetics comprise all things pleasurable, pleasing, and pretty.

Venus Archetypes need to be and feel like the brightest star in the room. Tell them regularly and often that they are beautiful, desired, and loved, and you shall be rewarded. You will find them working in arts and entertainment, where they literally take stage and expect an audience. They are the people cutting your hair, giving you a massage or a facial, and designing your boots and hats.

Just as Libras are symbolized by scales, so too does Venus represent balance, harmony, well-being, proportion, unity, partnership, evenness, and fairness. Libras are the diplomats and the peacekeepers. They fight for equality and fairness, balancing the scales in order to avoid conflict, war, fighting and incorrect balance.

Libras are compassionate, social, affectionate, and tender. They love to express their feelings. They are refined, delicate, cultured flowers that blossom with sex, desire, passion, lust, allure, and appeal. They are polite, good, and sweet, and the ambiance they create at home and at work reflects their heightened sense of fashion, style, and visual appeal.

Like their Libra and Taurus counterparts, Venus Archetypes are giving, creative, beautiful, balanced, harmonic, desirable, passionate, sympathetic, sentimental, aesthetic, artistic, and musical. Sure, on the down side they can be dependent, clingy, weepy, needy, passive, aloof, jealous, introverted, self-consciousness, high-maintenance, and narcissistic—but with one look, they can convince you to forgive them for most anything.

In Conclusion

Friday's Children live to please and are able to make friends and lovers wherever they go. Their brand is love. They are the Feminine, fertile and fruitful. They can live for sex, drugs, and rock and roll as well as the arts, dance, and (any type of) music. They live to be elegant and beautiful and to surround themselves with beautiful people and objects. They take great pride in their sense of fashion and often wear fabrics that invite touch. They know what's in fashion and in vogue—they know what they are wearing, as well as what everyone around them has on. Their clothes look and fit perfectly, like they do on a mannequin. They live with their secrets, and they love love stories. Your friends engaging in love triangles in the bedroom may very well be Venus Archetypes. Love is abundant, and is theirs to share.

The friend with a fabulous bathroom full of perfumes, bubble bath bottles, candles, and skin tonics, or shaving creams, razors, after shaves and colognes, was probably born on Friday—or a Venus Archetype. Their bathroom smells as yummy and inviting as their garden. They are open, affectionate, and sociable people, who others often label as "sweet." They are polite and courteous—which makes them excellent hosts or ambassadors—and they live to say thank you and please. They are charismatic and charming and make friends easily. They will say hello, smile at you, acknowledge you, or open or hold a door for you—this is a symbol of their openness.

As with any archetype, Venus Archetypes must be aware of their own strengths and weaknesses. They must recognize the fine line that divides the healthy positive powerful energy of attraction from destructive and dangerous behavior. Walking in beauty and desire feels good, but the darker and uglier side of life must be acknowledged in order for true growth, care, and action to occur.

It is easy to kick back and bask in the glow of a bright shining star, but more importantly, the light from a bright shining star can illuminate for each and every one of us what steps we need to take to heal ourselves and our planet. Beauty comes from within—it is a goodness and kindness that illuminates like the light bearing star of Venus ushers us into slumber and into facing our day. If we honor her regenerative and creative aspects, we remain beautiful inside, no matter our age, our phase, or our station—and we emanate love.

We are all looking for our soul mate, our true love, our person, our friend, our partner, our lover, and our spouse. From childhood friends, to high school and college sweethearts, to blind dates, friends of friends and coworkers, to someone we meet at the gym or online, we are searching for someone to bond with, to marry, to create a family with, and to age and die with. For some it comes easily, and for others it can be a challenge. If we look to the skies and the heavens, as the Ancients did, we see Venus guiding us on our search toward fate.

CHAPTER FOURTEEN

THE SATURN ARCHETYPE

Thus the heavens and the earth were completed in all their vast array.

By the seventh day God had finished the work he had been doing;
so on the seventh day he rested from all his work. Then God blessed the
seventh day and made it holy, because on it he rested from all the work
of creating that he had done.

—GENESIS

SATURDAY, 8:36 P.M. – 12:00 P.M.

A S THE LAST BIT OF SUNLIGHT SIGNALS THE DEATH OR THE END OF THE day, I ready myself for darkness, the day readies for rest and sleep. The cord is cut, the Moon rises, and the witching hour draws nearer. Iao Needle, a 1200-foot peak in the west Maui Mountains, looms in the distance. It is a sight to behold. For some, it is a fright, but I have always appreciated the dual nature of Hawaii and its mysteries, so in the silence, I imagine the warriors who once used the needle as a lookout. Iao Valley is my seventh wonder on Maui and the ideal place to "meditate with Saturn," reveal the meaning of Saturday ("Saturn's-Day")—the seventh day of creation, the seventh day of the week, and the day of the Saturn Planetary Archetype.

I am a small speck in this Saturnine setting. I, like Mother Goose's Saturday's Child, have worked hard, I have worked myself to the bone. I have worked myself almost to death, almost giving myself up to Saturn, the God of Death. It is a cloudy, cold, dark gray evening, and I allow thick feelings of gloom and moroseness to wash over me. Not all days on Maui are full of color, warmth, and sunshine—this is simply the way the world works.

We go through seasons, phases, moods, and cycles. The dark comes with the light, the good with the bad, the rainbows with the rain, and life with death.

So, I meditate on heaviness in this place, thinking of the cemeteries of Maui, particularly those that lie down the road and down Iao Stream. I think of the caves and the sinkholes filled with the bones of Hawaiians. In weather like this, I hear distant drums and wonder if someone is playing them, or if the island itself is rumbling. My awareness of how these Hawaiian Islands were made and how they continue to bubble up, grow, and harden, fuels my respect for the Earth's power and its continual changes. I think the Earth must be furious at us humans for the mistakes we have made as her stewards. I think Iao Needle looks as if it is trying to pierce the sky so that it will rain harder—shedding tears and grief, releasing its burden.

Created by years of entropy, natural chaos, and erosion, the needle is said to represent Kanaloa, the Hawaiian God of the underworld. Kanaloa rules boats, the ocean, and teaches magic. In the Iao Valley, I open myself to whatever magic comes my way. Like the octopus that often represents Kanaloa, I reach out with all of my tentacles, or senses, so that I can ponder Saturday, Saturn, and the Saturn Planetary Archetype.

Seated amidst a patch of Ti plants, I feel protected. In cultures across the Pacific Ocean, from New Guinea to New Zealand and from Bali to the Philippines, the Ti plant has been revered for centuries. Its roots are used in healing tonics and tinctures and its leaves are said to hold souls and fend off evil and malevolent spirits. Wearing Ti leaves induces spiritual awakening and connection. The Polynesians brought the Ti plant to Hawaii centuries ago.

The Ti leaf in Hawaiian culture has multiple uses and purposes. It is used as roof thatching and to wrap the flesh of animals—to cook meat—in traditional underground ovens. Once worn only by Hawaiian shamans and kings, these leaves are now also worn in traditional hula dancers' skirts. Some Hawaiians carry a leaf in their pocket or purse for good luck and good health.

Ti is used in funeral leis and in burials, so that the deceased may transition to the other world and rest in peace. Offerings to the dead and to the

Gods are often bound in Ti leaves and placed at burial plots, tombstones, and known spiritual vortexes around the islands. Ti also brings a state of rest-fulness to the living, and is often used in tandem with meditation. Whenever I touch the Ti plant, make a sacrificial bundle or basket with its leaves, or rest near it, I am instantly calmed and put into a frame of mind of gratefulness. I accept that there is magic I have little or no access to, and I understand I have the magic of my own upbringing, present, and future.

I remember learning as a boy the history of the sacred and scarred, the bold and the bloody Iao Valley. This valley is the site of one of the deadliest battles in Hawaiian history, the 1790 Battle of Kepaniwai. In this fight, King Kamehmeha I of the Big Island of Hawaii led just over one thousand fierce warriors to overthrow Maui, while its king, King Kahekili, was visiting Oahu. Under the Iao Needle, so many Maui natives were killed that their corpses blocked the stream, resulting in the "damning of the waters," which translates as Kepaniwai.

But, out of this chaos came order and the unification of Hawaii under one rule. The ancients believed the mortal remains, or the bones and skulls of the deceased, especially kings, contained mana, or divine power, and therefore these bones were treated with respect. These remains were guarded so they could pass power and control onto their descendants, keeping struc-ture and control in their families for generations to come. Bone is harder and stronger than muscle. Bone preserves and stands the test of time.

Iao Needle stands over this story of blood, death, rot, and decay. Some say they still find an 18th-century tooth or a bone in the soil, but of course, nobody dares to remove a thing! This is a place of chaos and curses, but it is also where the Wailuku Stream starts its course toward Wailuku town.

In Wailuku, you find official city government business being conducted. The streets are packed with court buildings and offices of law and order. Judges and attorneys dine over seafood lunches. City planning and building board members and commissioners grab a Spam Musubi. A police station and a fire station sit amongst construction and development companies. People who work for work force development, mechanics and electricians, and those good citizens running for office saddle up aside those who work in longevity health centers, mortuaries, crematoriums, and funeral homes and parlors. In Wailuku, one will find the backbone of society and those who truly "work hard for a living" to serve and protect others, to give us a base and structure to work up from, to benefit the community and society as a whole.

Saturn Archetypes are the pawns of life and the servants of society. Although known as the malefic planet, there is no other Archetype that will do more to solve our most serious problems. This archetype is born to serve and will fall on the sword or the sickle for others. Because they are at the bottom, there is nowhere to go but up, and moving up is their goal—through hard work and the building of relationships and contracts, through social events and through marriage, they strive and thrive.

Saturn represents long-term planning, social hierarchies, and structure, as well as one's duty and responsibility to such. They are serious and ambitious about life and careers, especially in the domains of authority and control. They are government and government workers, politicians, and anyone that serves and protects, from fire and police, to judges and lawyers, to teachers and educators. They are planners, engineers, builders, social workers, laborers, and grunts.

On one hand, Saturn has the responsibility of serving society and on the other, the task of attending to each and every trial and tribulation. To serve society means to lay its foundation and to uphold it. Justice, civility, and obedience are key Saturn Archetype values, and all are served on the streets and in the court systems. Wrongs are righted by Saturn babies. Justice, revenge, clemency, and mercy are served.

When not at work, Saturn Archetypes love reading and watching TV shows about society and social issues—from daytime tabloid talk shows where people air their dirty laundry, to small claims court and judge/jury dramas. Those hospital dramas are favorites, as are all fire and police and law and order shows. "Be seated," and "all rise as we render the verdict" and "your word can be held against you" can be heard in the living rooms of those under the influence of Saturn. They are into difficulty, challenges, obstacles, things that go wrong, suffering, distress, affliction, and life's lessons. Saturn is the teacher, the taskmaster, and the strict authority figure that stands for responsibility, discipline, rules, and lessons. Saturn is burdened with worry, stress, despair, the heaviness of life and all that it has to teach us. Saturn carries the scars of life, mentally, emotionally and physically.

In Iao Valley, we Curious George types who satisfy our souls with not only history, but also with anthropology and archaeology, used to visit what is known as "rainbow man," one of Hawaii's oldest petroglyphs. The man on the ancient rock carving stands beneath an arc, which is said to represent responsibility, and the weight of responsibility. Several Hawaiian clubs and organizations now use this image to symbolize humanity's role in protecting the Earth from those who mean to destroy it, namely greedy humans. As a child, we took more than one school field trip to visit and discuss "rainbow man," but now, a sign reading: Kapu, or Keep Out, protects the stone from being further defaced or damaged.

Practicality, reason, and reliability are where Saturday's Children feel most comfortable, capable, and confident. Give them a task that they can crystallize, and they will. Give them a career or a hobby with structure, and they will never leave abandon it. Saturn governs ambition, career, authority, and hierarchy, so loosey-goosey open-spaced work environments might cause them stress.

They appreciate conforming social structures, duty, discipline, and responsibility. They look good in a uniform, and are drawn to careers that require them.

Saturn represents long-term planning, perhaps because it is such a long way from the sun. The Saturn Archetype understands time and its freedoms and limitations. Overseeing long-range projects that others would quickly and easily get bored with is Saturn's secret joy!

The Saturn Archetype goes through life as the servant, scaffolding and supporting society and social order. Chaos gives them the willies, because chaos indicates a disrespect of time, or worse, a full-blown dismantling of time. Oh no, time is of the essence, and time must be well spent. So, the Saturday's Child Saturn Archetype happily seeks out tasks, and then always works through them to completion.

They go through life with a unique awareness of death. The friend that dresses in black and never misses a funeral is likely a Saturn Archetype. The friend who works in a hospital, a hospice, a home for the elderly, a morgue, or in forensics, may be a Saturday's child. Death does not phase them the way if phases others, because they see it as part of the wheel of life. Death is natural.

Still, in order not to waste a day before dying, they go through life with their calendars and planners within reach. They sit on as many boards as they can and they plan, plan, plan ways to keep society functioning, just, and whole. Even with the lawbreakers and chaos-makers of the world, the Saturn Archetype sees what can be fixed, and gets to work on a rehabilitation plan.

Saturn's interest in or acceptance of death may be conscious or subconscious. But either way, death is an essence of their life, if not the essence. For Saturn, all qualities arise from this trust in Cronus, and in what takes place between being born, aging and dying. Death is never seen as the absolute ending point, but as a step in getting rid of what is no longer of service or helpful. Death opens up space for more birth!

Perhaps because of its association with the gavel, judgment, or punishment, Saturn has many friends of the dark, of the night, of the gloomy and sorrowful. The witch in her black coat and hat, broom and black cat in tow cackles, "I'll get you, my pretty." The black crow with its long black sickle shape beak stares from the winter tree that is bare of leaves. The Grim Reaper, Father Time, Rip Van Winkle, Doctors of Death, the old limping crone, all evil spirits and omens that come from the witches' cauldron are associated with Saturn.

They are the sheriff with a mustache, the enforcer, the punisher, or anyone who seeks revenge, mercy or retribution. Other times the prosecutor or the defendant, the gavel and the verdict. The judge, the jury and the executioner all serve the ringed planet.

But, out of the salt of the earth, out of the dirt, grease, and grime of the laborers and blue-collar workers' collars, comes the most positive influence on society. Work builds character. Here, we establish order and infrastructure of cities, states, and countries. Here, we find the turning of the clocks, the wheels and hands of time, from hours, to minutes and seconds. Here we find the mundane punching of the timecards and timeclocks, some called "Chronos."

Saturn works through life with the "Lead Bones of Hard Work, Structure and Society of the Servant" and the spleen and skeletal system activated with the Power of "Order." When all is functioning well, the Saturn Archetype is serious, ordered, controlled, and lawful. They strive toward justice and participate in social work, social events, and social planning. They pay attention to cleanliness, longevity, and time. When the lead bones are broken and the spleen and skeletal system are weak, the Saturn Archetype loses their sense of order, and the body can give into mental diseases of stress, worry and be hypochondriacs or produce physical ailments of the spleen, elimination and intestinal toxicity. They can be quite anal, both good and bad. They may experience degenerative diseases of the bones, tissues, joints, ligaments, knees, ankles, and teeth.

1. The Seven Days of Creation and of the Week

We know how busy God was on Friday, making all his creatures great and small and ensuring we all had a partner to be fruitful and multiply with. If a mere mortal had done all that work in one day, they would be dead by the end of it. But God worked his wonders, and then he said, "Time out," and called down Saturn to rule over and influence things. Saturday is a day to "rest," but it is also symbolic of Saturn, and therefore of "eternal rest," or R.I.P, rest in peace, or death.

Saturday is a holy day of rest. Yes, so is Sunday and depending on your religion or outlook on life, Sunday might be your Sabbath. Either way though, most of us agree that weekends are for play, rest, and all things non-work related. Not long ago, it was illegal to work on Saturdays, and those who did invoked an ill omen, or bad luck. Now, Saturday is often a social day of marriage or "until death do us part."

Even nomads travel for six days and rest on the seventh as they know our brains, our bones, and our bodies enjoy a time out, and that time out allows us to renew and repair all that we might have broken down or stretched a bit too thin. The seventh day brings the completion of an age, time or cycle. It stands for the end of the sands of time flowing in an hourglass, or the last tick or tock of a clock. All hail Saturn!

2. The Seven Naked Eye Planets

Although we all have the capacity and urge to work hard, only some of us can work as hard as Saturn. Saturn, last in the Chaldean order of the naked eye planets and the furthest planet from Sun, is dark and heavy. Its surface is cold, icy, and uninviting. In our imagination, it is the land of the banished and the dead. Saturn marks the boundary of our visual universe, the cold and the dark, a place of no return.

I associate Saturn, the slowest planet, with burdens and duty. In its rings, I see dark rings under someone's eyes, or rings of a cut tree, or a way to measure time, aging, decay, and death. When I see someone wearing a ring on every finger or bracelet after bracelet shimmering on their wrists, I think of Saturn and its icy dense rings. When someone is having a birthday and I say "throw another ring around Saturn," they usually don't know what I mean. Saturn is associated with Chronos, and so my mind automatically goes to dark stories of castration, attempted murder, and a father eating his offspring.

But of course, in the word "Saturn" is the word "turn." All of life moves in cycles, and the flip side of darkness and cold is light and warmth. A grandparent dies and a grandchild is born. The wheel turns on its axis and around its orbit, just as Saturn does.

3. The Gods of Myth

Just as there are many ways to keep time, Saturn goes by many names as well. From Chronos (Greek), Saturn (Roman), Kronos, Saturnus, we know Saturn, also as Father Time and the Grim Reaper, the God of time, death, control, structure, law, order, law and order, entropy, limitation, constriction, duty, service, responsibility, aging, and longevity.

Cronus, from where we get the word chronological, was the son of Uranus, who ruled Heaven, and of Gaea, our sweet Mother Earth. As the God of Time and Death, Cronus, aka Saturn, ruled ages, aging and agriculture. He managed the sowing of seeds and the harvest. In art, he is often depicted as an old man with a sickle. This God rules over our very sustenance. He also rules over our souls. And he has a cruel and turbulent side: With his sickle, Cronus either castrated or killed his own father, thus triggering the cycle of death.

As he aged, Cronus gave life, fathering children of his own. Considering his history, many predicted and warned that if he were not extremely careful, he would meet the exact same fate as his dad. To avoid this embarrassment (or repeat act, or awful moment before dying where one realizes his own spawn are out to annihilate him), he eats his own kids.

Zeus though, born in secret and sent to Crete, escapes this nightmare. His caretakers surround his crib with some goats and dancers, to mask his cries. After he has grown up and put on muscle, he then presents himself to Cronus, giving him an emetic that causes him to vomit back up the children he ate. Zeus has siblings again and essentially they all say, "Shoo, Dad!" to Cronus and send him off to life in prison.

The message with Saturn is not as bold as, "Don't eat your babies," but it is a lesson in being mindful that you may "reap what you sow." Whatever you put your time into, will return to you. So yes, don't eat your babies, or they will come (back to life) for you and for revenge.

4. The Archangels or Guardian Angels

Saturday's angel, as you might imagine, is concerned with time, tears, the burden of life, and death, and karma. Cassiel can be called upon when each minute of each hour feels impossibly slow, as in after a breakup or when someone has died and the grief changes the way an hour feels. At the same time, when things are moving too quickly and there are not enough hours in a day to multitask and get stuff done, Cassiel can be asked to spread his wings and spread calm. This angel covers you while you weep, and encourages you to feel all your feelings and let them all out, because crying is a sacred purge and a healing act. They can also bring Cassiel to their side whenever their loved ones are exiting the land of the living and entering the land of the dead. This angel is here for us at all mileposts on our journey from birth to death.

5. The Seven Classical Metals

The heaviest and densest metal, lead was used by the Egyptians in weights, sinkers, and pipes. Agricultural output and gold were measured and divvied up using lead; fish were caught; and water was moved and distributed.

Lead allows humankind to structure society—we sketch, plan, and design buildings and landscapes with pencils. We scribble out our laws with pencils. Dreams are journaled and inventions dreamed, in pencil. Teachers instruct students to take notes (sure now with laptops and handheld devices), in their classrooms using the mighty pencil. Lessons are taught with lead.

Lead is the bullet that sometimes is used to uphold the law, but also to "hit the bone" and commit murder. There is darkness and death in lead. Lead poisoning, which often does not manifest until it reaches a high level of concentration in the blood, sometimes starts out as fatigue. One feels sluggish or constipated, mentally confused or moody and gloomy. Lead in paint and in the production of cans for canned goods is outlawed in the United States, but older homes and buildings still contain lead-based paint and generate lead-laden dust. Lead is not only used in paint, but to paint the lines of the roads and curbs. Lead sets the rules of the road and controls traffic. "Follow the line, stay within the line, don't cross the line," are all ways to ensure we obey the rules that Saturn is casting from Above. Serious exposure to lead can result in sterility (think of Cronus castrating his father!) and death. Lead is used to line caskets to preserve and slow decomposition.

6. The Seven Vortexes, or Chakras and Organ Systems

At the base of our spine lies the seventh vortex, also known appropriately, as the base vortex, the spinal vortex, or the order vortex. This center represents Saturn, and guides all aspects of our lives that necessitate structure, order, and control.

Physically and physiologically, the spleen, the skeletal system, the bones, joints, cartilage and teeth work under the influence of the seventh chakra.

When all is running as it should here, structure, control, alignment and hard work comes easy. We greet the day with enthusiasm and determination to get the job done, and to get it done well. Worries fall away, because we know that any challenge can be met and conquered with an action plan. Our spine holds together and holds up upright and when we work from our Saturn-influenced chakra, we stand tall and confident. Nothing shakes our resolve and tasks, though there may be many, flow smoothly. All processes and systems are efficient. We can knock down walls to get things done. We are hard and strong as bone and teeth.

A blockage in this chakra results in the feeling that corpses are dead in the water. Nobody is getting the job done, people are dropping like flies. Obstacles seem insurmountable and all outcomes feel doomed.

Chronic neglect or overstimulation of the seventh vortex results in dis-eases (which I like to break down to "dis" and "eases") of the spleen. A healthy spleen is needed to clean toxins and poisons out of the body so they do not calcify in the blood and bones. Mentally and emotionally, worry, stress, and pessimism take over. Seriousness and tightness take control of the reins and it is hard for the sufferer to "let loose," and to literally have a healthy bowel movement. The need to control everything and everyone brings about unnecessarily high and undeserved levels of criticalness. Being too fixed in one's ways is the path to rigidness, entropy, and death. The skeletal system softens and arthritis blows up in those who take Saturn to the extreme, and who overwork, overthink, and overstress. The mental and emotional scars and scar tissues of life are hardened by Saturn as the task master.

Humor or laughter is great medicine for the out-of-whack Saturn chakra. So is any activity that forces you to ground yourself, balance, and work your core, such as walking barefoot on rough or tactile surfaces.

7. Planetary Age and Hours Cycles

We spend ages fifty-six to sixty-three in our Saturn years. This is the last of the seven ages we experience before we "die" and return to our second Moon age, or cycle. These years, though they don't feel like it for many in this day and age, traditionally were considered our "old age" years. And though many of us can no longer imagine retiring the way our grandparents and parents did, while they were in their sixties, it used to be that in our Saturn years we began to tidy up the loose ends of our career and plan for easier days, filled with hobbies, friends, and time spent with younger additions to the family.

These are the years we wish we had more time and more years. Life slows down. Life is structured, stable, and predictable, and there are fewer surprises because we have "been there, done that." Now, we ponder or dwell on death and the afterlife. We question what we will leave behind in terms of wealth and reputation. We worry about our assets and set wills and estates to decide what goes where. And we realize we will soon come face-to-face with our own personal test and evaluation of how we spent our precious time. Some say we will be judged one last time. There is comfort in this age too, as many trials and tribulations we once fretted over, for no real reason or value, come to an end. And then we contract, shrink, calcify, and die, hopefully, in peace.

The Saturn Planetary Hour is from 8:36 p.m. to 12:00 p.m., as we digest our meal, kick up our feet and read a book or watch TV, or put ourselves to bed and pull up the covers, we mindfully prepare our bodies for slumber and rest as the day dies. We review our day, think about our tomorrow, and enter the world that only exists when we close and rest our eyes, in both life and death, shutting the light out.

8. The Seven Lost Symbols

Saturn's symbol, ♄ , is the cross, or the Cross of Death. It is the cross and sickle, the cross over the sickle, the Sickle of Death, the Sickle of the Grim Reaper, or the Sickle that is used to chop off the heads of the dead after they have been judged. Saturn put an end to his father's ability to produce life with a sickle; but, of course, the sickle is a key tool in agricultural history, it was used to reap the harvest to ultimately feed and ensure the survival of a growing global human population. And it was also used to reap and harvest the souls of the dead. Go to a cemetery and imagine the Grim Reaper holding a sickle in his boney hands and you will know and understand this symbol stands for time and for the test of time, which for us, ends in judgment and death.

9. The Twelve Sun Signs of Contemporary Astrology

Saturn Archetypes have a lot in common with Capricorns and Sagittarians. These are the stoics of the world, and they have to work at not becoming stuck. They are the hard workers, the strict ones, so you'll often find them designing society—they are lawyers and law clerks, judges and court transcribers, police and civil servants. Friends of the lead pencil, yes, they are teachers and educators.

Symbolized by the goat, Capricorns are dedicated and determined servants that work ambitiously to reach their personal goals, their summit, or the summit. They might ascend to the top social classes, breaking through and knocking down walls and challenges along the way. The Saturn Archetype, like any good Capricorn, minds and appreciates the principles of limitations, restrictions, and boundaries as they take on many tasks, projects, and responsibilities in order to reap the benefits. Parenting is one job that requires us to call upon Saturn often, no matter what planet is our primary governor!

Aquarians are symbolized by the Water Bearer, or Carrier, and they carry the burden, the weight, the duty, the responsibility, and the burden of us all. They are ever mindful of structure, control, order, law, and justice. They hold up the base, the bottom, the foundation of all matters with their calendars and planners. They, like Saturday's children, can be unemotional, sorrowful, and morose in their role as the responsible, dutiful servant. Aquarians are social and civil servants of law and order and they protect and serve in order to make things more equal, fair and just.

Living always aware of death, for the Capricorn and Aquarius of the Saturn Archetype, is what limits their options and is the reason that they choose a career path and any outside hobbies carefully. All Saturday Children do, they do with deep thought, deep focus, and deep commitment. In an office environment, Saturn sometimes mistakenly assumes that everyone has come to a meeting fully prepared. Straying off topic from the agenda roils their blood, and if too many deviations are made, Saturn will suddenly turn heavy, grave, and serious. The weight of Saturn will fill the room and for the most part, everyone will fall in line because "this is not a game", so serious they are, dedicated to their career ambitions,

Though many of us associate Saturday with the weekend and with running off and being carefree, the Saturday Child is often trapped by their own seriousness or "Debby Downer-ness." The Saturn Archetype is not everybody's friend—one or two trustworthy, loyal, responsible, and reliable people will do. When trust is broken, forgiving is possible, but forgetting, never. "Respect" is a key word in the Saturn Archetype's vocabulary.

In Conclusion

Saturday's children are work and career oriented. At risk of working themselves to the bone, or of becoming so rigid they risk early rigor mortis, the Saturn Archetype literally has to let a load off. Saturn friends, do please stop trying to carry the weight of lead and the world on your shoulders! We need you to keep us structured, sane, and safe. We enjoy your cleanliness, neatness, borderline OCD-ness. We are sorry that we sometimes come home and throw our jackets on the floor and leave dirty dishes in the sink. Our calendars look like chicken scratch and we realize you sit there biting your nails resisting the urge to erase and rewrite our daily lives.

Saturday's Children, do keep keeping our social calendars moving, and be sure to come out with us sometimes too, to keep yourselves loose and limber. Nobody can follow all of the rules all of the time. Never forget that experts are now proving the value of time off doing nothing. Doctors in fact prescribe "hammock time," and daydreaming. If you pencil this in on your calendar, follow through.

In life, Saturn, the control freak and authoritarian, points out each person's responsibility and task. They are controlling and strictly in control. Saturn reminds everyone what they agreed to do and lends a hand to complete the task, but Saturn also reveals one's accomplishments or failures. A deal is a deal, and a word is also a deal. One doesn't just talk, but does whatever it takes to achieve the task at hand. Our duty is our weight and it is as heavy as lead.

You may grind your teeth. You may grin and bear it. You may experience despair, negativity, and pessimism. Metaphorically, you live furthest of all archetypes from the Sun, so it is natural you will tend to dwell in sorrow and moroseness. You live in a world of all things legal and contracts—business deals and personal ones-while you contract, harden, and solidify. You are the workers and those who don't work. You are the law and the law breakers. You are the architect of structure and the crafters of chaos; you sit on your planning boards, community service boards, your law exams and boards, bored with aging. You subside to learn life lessons and teach us ours.

The aches in your spleen, teeth, bones, joints, and ligaments all stem from the fact you work too hard, play the long game with every game, and rarely give yourself a break. Stones, calcifications, scars, poisons, toxins, minerals, calcium, small intestines and problems with constipation and elimination are the crosses you, dear Saturn Archetype must battle or bear.

But as is the case with every planetary archetype, the power to fulfill your highest role in the time you have been gifted on Earth, resides within you. What more can you discover about Saturn and the origins of who you are? How can you face your influences, good and bad, dark and light, and restructure them to better suit your needs and goals? A master at planning for others and following through on multiple and varied tasks, dear Saturday's Child, how will you now follow through on Project You?

Outro

THE SEVEN PLANETS, OR "PLANETOS," OR "WANDERING STARS," ARE THE Seven Wonders of the universe. I am a Seven Wonder, you are a Seven Wonder—we are all Seven Wonders! I am a Day of Creation, a Day of the Week, a Planetary God/Goddess, an Angel, a planet, a metal, a symbol and one of the Seven Ancient Planetary Archetypes. We are created in their image—As Above, so below, as in Heaven, so on earth, Macrocosm and microcosm!

This is why we have a seven-day week:

Sunday, Monday, Tuesday, Wednesday, Thursday, Friday, Saturday

This is why we have seven days of Creation!

If we look at the Seven Planets and assign One Verse to each, we would see that the Sun, the Father, is exactly what you would expect the Father to be: open-hearted, full-hearted, expressive, outward, enriching, positive and soulful; a loyal provider of warmth, light, compassion, and lively creative energy. The Father teaches us about our self, our ego, and our pride. We learn from him who we are. We form with him our inspirations and aspirations and ideas about how we will shine our light in the world.

The Moon, or the Mother, is exactly what you would expect the Mother to be. She provides a home from conception to birth, from infancy and throughout life. Under her, we feel cared for, protected. We are nursed and taught. We discover our internal emotions and feelings, and we develop our perception and awareness. We hone our instincts and reflect on our past and history.

Mars, or the Male, is the warrior, full of testosterone and adrenalin. This archetype is physical, aggressive, competitive, and domineering. Mars is in it to win, to fight, to start wars, and to be the alpha. Masculine, sexual, violent, angry, passionate, fiery, and skilled, Mars excels at leadership, athletics, and battles of all kinds.

Venus, or the Female, is the lover and the ruler of beauty, art, openness, sex, and affections. Relationships, friendship and reproduction are her domain; love, peace, harmony, balance, and well-being are her forte.

Jupiter, or the Ruler, is the spiritual, religious, and financial ruler. This archetype is expansive and full of faith, righteousness, holiness, power, authority, morals, values, and dogmas. Abundance, prosperity, money, wealth, luck, accumulation and food and diet fall under the spell of the Jupiter Archetype. Here, we find the creator of laws, the protector of the environment, the conservationist, philanthropist, and humanitarian.

Saturn, or the Servant, serves and protects via law and order, planning, control, structure and infrastructure. This archetype works hard to provide and maintain the foundation of a civil society. Carrying the burden and the seriousness, the duty and the load, Saturn has no problem handling the weight and the responsibility of the world.

Mercury, the Communicator, dwells in—you name it—language, words, reading, writing, science, technology, reason, ration, logic, intelligence, and intellect. The Mercury Archetype is the changeling, the wild card, the in-between, the middleman, the jokester, the jester, the entertainer, the traveler, the trader, the performer and the wind and air.

As Above, so below!

The Planetary Archetype Chart

("The Philosopher's Stone")

Planet	Sun	Moon	Mars	Mercury	Jupiter	Venus	Saturn
Time	Sun	Mon	Tues	Wed	Thurs	Fri	Sat
12:00 am - 3:26 am	☉ ♂	☽ ☿	♂ ♃	☿ ♀	♃ ♄	♀ ☉	♄ ☽
3:26 am - 6:52 am	☉ ☉	☽ ☽	♂ ♂	☿ ☿	♃ ♃	♀ ♀	♄ ♄
6:52 am - 10:18 am	☉ ♀	☽ ♄	♂ ☉	☿ ☽	♃ ♂	♀ ☿	♄ ♃
10:18 am - 1:44 pm	☉ ☿	☽ ♃	♂ ♀	☿ ♄	♃ ☉	♀ ☽	♄ ♂
1:44 pm - 5:10 pm	☉ ☽	☽ ♂	♂ ☿	☿ ♃	♃ ♀	♀ ♄	♄ ☉
5:10 pm - 8:36 pm	☉ ♄	☽ ☉	♂ ☽	☿ ♂	♃ ☿	♀ ♃	♄ ♀
8:36 pm - 12:00 am	☉ ♃	☽ ♀	♂ ♄	☿ ☉	♃ ☽	♀ ♂	♄ ☿

THE SEVEN ANCIENT PLANETARY ARCHETYPES SUMMARY

Planet	Moon	Mercury	Venus	Sun	Mars	Jupiter	Saturn
Symbol	☽	☿	♀	☉	♂	♃	♄
Day	Monday	Wednesday	Friday	Sunday	Tuesday	Thursday	Saturday
Metals	Silver (Ag)	Mercury (hG)	Copper (Cu)	Gold (Au)	Iron (Fe)	Tin (Sn)	Lead (Pb)
Major Organs	Brain	Lungs	Kidney	Heart	Blood	Liver	Spleen
Major Systems	Nervous	Respiratory	Urinary	Circulatory	Immune	Metabolic	Structural
Minor Organs	Stomach	Nerves	Genitals	Blood	Gallbladder	Pancreas	Bones
Minor Systems	Fertility, Breasts	Throat, Ears	Ovaries/ Testes, Veins	Eyes, Vision	Adrenals, Arteries	Large Intestine, Thyroid	Small Intestine, Ligaments
Tissues	Marrow	Lymph	Mucous	Plasma	Muscles	Fat	Joints
Functions	Emotions, Feelings, Dreams	Intellect, Speech, Hearing	Sex, Affections, Taste	Warmth, Vitality, Focus	Will, Defense, Fitness	Energy, Appetite, Digestion	Structure, Alignment, Elimination
Strengths	Perception, Clarity	Adaptability, Coordination	Resonance, Well-Being	Aspiration, Inspiration	Strength, Survival	Growth, Accumalation	Control, Order
Weakness	Ignorance, Fears	Instability, Sensitivity	Desires, Affections	Pride, Ego	Anger, Aggression	Greed, Insecurity	Worry, Pessimism
Zodiac Signs	Cancer	Gemini, Virgo	Taurus, Libra	Leo	Aries, Scorpio	Pisces, Sagitarius	Aquarius, Capricorn
Archetype	Mother	Communicator	Lover	Father	Warrior	Ruler	Servant

JORDAN STARK

J ORDAN STARK WAS RAISED ON THE ISLAND OF MAUI, HAWAII, WHERE HE attended a Rudolph Steiner Waldorf School, located on the gentle slopes of Haleakala, Maui. Here Jordan was first introduced to the ancient creation stories of all cultures around the world, complete with all their myths, legends and folklore. After Haleakala School he attended Seabury Hall high school and developed a passion for classical and symbolic literature. His education continued with his studies of anthropology and archaeology, with an emphasis on Egypt, the Aztecs and Mayans at the University of Colorado in Boulder.

After college, Jordan pursued this knowledge on his own, working his way through ancient cultures, from the ancient age, to the old age as well as our modern and contemporary age. These studies brought him full circle back to the beginning of our search for knowledge and wisdom within the creation stories of our ancient ancestors. Fascinated by Hermes Trismegistus, considered by many to be the first scribe of God, his creation story, as well as the creation of the seven-day week, Jordan searched for our first answers to our first questions.

Jordan has over 25 years as an astral-anthropologist, studying and applying this ancient planetary astrology. He knows what it is like to be Friday-born, and a Venus Archetype, complete with her mental, emotional and physical traits, qualities and attributes. Jordan has spent many years proving what Hermes once said: "Tis true without lying, certain and most true. That which is below is like that which is above and that which is above is like that which is below to do the miracles of only one thing." That "one thing" is our Creation Story—how we are created in the image of our Ruling Planet.